TRANSNATIONAL CORPORATIONS AND DEVELOPING COUNTRIES:
New Policies for a Changing World Economy

CED

A Statement by the Research and
Policy Committee of the
Committee for Economic Development
April 1981

Library of Congress Cataloging in Publication Data

Committee for Economic Development. Research and Policy Committee.
  Transnational corporations and developing countries.

  Includes bibliographical references.
    1. Underdeveloped areas—International business enterprises.
  2. Underdeveloped areas—Industry and state.
  I. Title.
  HD2755.5.C635   1981   338.8′881724   81-3277
  ISBN 0-87186-072-4 (pbk.)   AACR2
  ISBN 0-87186-772-9 (lib. bdg.)

First printing: April 1981
Paperbound: $5.00
Library binding: $6.50
Printed in the United States of America
Design: Stead, Young & Rowe, Inc.

COMMITTEE FOR ECONOMIC DEVELOPMENT
477 Madison Avenue, New York, N.Y. 10022
1700 K Street, N.W., Washington, D.C. 20006

CONTENTS

TRANSNATIONAL CORPORATIONS AND DEVELOPING COUNTRIES:
New Policies for a Changing World Economy

RESPONSIBILITY FOR CED STATEMENTS ON NATIONAL POLICY

The Committee for Economic Development is an independent research and educational organization of two hundred business executives and educators. CED is nonprofit, nonpartisan, and nonpolitical. Its purpose is to propose policies that will help to bring about steady economic growth at high employment and reasonably stable prices, increase productivity and living standards, provide greater and more equal opportunity for every citizen, and improve the quality of life for all. A more complete description of CED is to be found on page 88.

All CED policy recommendations must have the approval of the Research and Policy Committee, trustees whose names are listed on page vii. This Committee is directed under the bylaws to "initiate studies into the principles of business policy and of public policy which will foster the full contribution by industry and commerce to the attainment and maintenance" of the objectives stated above. The bylaws emphasize that "all research is to be thoroughly objective in character, and the approach in each instance is to be from the standpoint of the general welfare and not from that of any special political or economic group." The Committee is aided by a Research Advisory Board of leading social scientists and by a small permanent professional staff.

The Research and Policy Committee is not attempting to pass judgement on any pending specific legislative proposals; its purpose is to urge careful consideration of the objectives set forth in this statement and of the best means of accomplishing those objectives.

Each statement is preceded by extensive discussions, meetings, and exchanges of memoranda. The research is undertaken by a subcommittee, assisted by advisors chosen for their competence in the field under study. The members and advisors of the subcommittee that prepared this statement are listed on page viii.

The full Research and Policy Committee participates in the drafting of findings and recommendations. Likewise, the trustees on the drafting subcommittee vote to approve or disapprove a policy statement, and they share with the Research and Policy Committee the privilege of submitting individual comments for publication, as noted on pages vii and viii and on the appropriate page of the text of the statement.

Except for the members of the Research and Policy Committee and the responsible subcommittee, the recommendations presented herein are not necessarily endorsed by other trustees or by the advisors, contributors, staff members, or others associated with CED.

RESEARCH AND POLICY COMMITTEE

PURPOSE OF THIS STATEMENT

At a time when developing countries are demanding a greater say in their own political, social, and economic destinies, it seems appropriate to reexamine the controversial role of transnational corporations in the Third World. Despite public rhetoric calling for international action to "tame the multinationals," it is becoming increasingly apparent that private enterprise, with its capital, technological capabilities, and managerial know-how, is the best hope for future Third World economic development. As more and more developed countries reduce their foreign aid, in real terms, to emerging nations, the need for mutually advantageous private investment will be vital, particularly for oil-poor lower-income countries.

INCREASING THE MUTUAL GAINS

Despite highly publicized conflicts, both transnational corporations and developing countries are making tremendous strides in improving their day-to-day working relationships. Nevertheless, tensions remain. The purpose of this policy statement by the Committee for Economic Development (CED) is to clarify the main issues that have arisen between transnational enterprises and host countries in the Third World and to propose policies to ease remaining tensions and increase the mutual gains.

In considering this subject, the Committee benefited greatly from the results of an extensive survey of the role of foreign direct investment in the Third World that was sponsored jointly by CED and its counterpart organizations in Australia, France, Germany, Japan, Sweden, and the United Kingdom. The study, *Foreign Enterprise in Developing Countries*, by Dr. Isaiah Frank, found that as transnational corporations are becoming more sensitive to the political, social, and economic needs of the developing countries, Third World nations are, in turn, becoming more confident and competent in dealing with foreign firms.

The study was based on in-depth interviews with top operating personnel from over 400 transnational affiliates and on discussions and conferences with representatives of the developing countries, including government officials and staff members of United Nations agencies. Because of such personal contacts, the research study was able to cut through many of the myths and misconceptions that have become associated with transnational operations in the Third World and to pinpoint ways in which companies and host countries are learning to accommodate each other in their practical everyday relations.

The study also provided the Committee with an invaluable base upon which to develop a comprehensive set of policies to guide transnational corporations, their host and home countries, and various international agencies in improving relationships between host governments and foreign affiliates in the Third World. A brief discussion of *Foreign Enterprise in Developing Countries* is presented in Appendix A, page 72.

AN INTERDEPENDENT WORLD ECONOMY

From its inception in 1942, CED has labored to build a consensus on policies that promote economic growth and development. CED's most recent policy statements, *Fighting Inflation and Rebuilding a Sound Economy* (1980), *Stimulating Technological Progress* (1980), *Helping Insure Our Energy Future* (1979), and *Redefining Government's Role in the Market System* (1979), focused on the network of interrelated problems that are stifling the productive capabilities of the U.S. economy. At the same time, the Committee recognizes that no one nation's economy exists in a vacuum. High inflation, lagging productivity growth, and soaring energy costs are global as well as domestic issues that must be examined within the context of an interdependent world economy.

CED's concern with international economic issues can also be traced to its beginnings. CED's first chairman, Paul G. Hoffman, who was the first administrator of the Marshall Plan and who also spearheaded the United Nations Development Program, put the Committee firmly on the track of promoting international growth and economic development. In recent years, CED has devoted a number of policy statements to an examination of U.S. government policies that could contribute to Third World economic and social development. In *Assisting Development in Low-Income Countries* (1969) and *Development Assistance to Southeast Asia* (1970), the Committee studied the role of the U.S. government in providing development assistance to emerging nations and in encouraging private investment in those countries. A 1975 policy statement, *International Economic Consequences of High-Priced Energy*, developed jointly by CED and six of its counterpart organizations in Europe, Japan, and Australia, examined the effects of the 1973 OPEC oil price shocks on low-income, energy-importing nations. That statement once again urged the developed nations to encourage private investment in developing countries in order to contribute to the long-term economic growth of the Third World.

The present statement represents a departure from previous CED reports on assistance to the Third World. Rather than concentrating on the role of U.S. government policy, the statement focuses primarily on the actions that host-country governments and transnational corporations can take together in order to promote a better business partnership. The Committee hopes that such direct interaction can simultaneously help to meet the pressing economic and social needs of developing countries, improve the operating environment for transnational affiliates, and contribute to a stronger world economy.

ACKNOWLEDGMENTS

On behalf of the Research and Policy Committee, I express deep appreciation for the tireless efforts of Edmund B. Fitzgerald, president of Northern Telecom Inc., who, as chairman of the Subcommittee on Economic Relations Between Industrial and Less Developed Countries, provided the astute leadership to guide both the initial research report and this policy statement from inception to conclusion. Our thanks also go to the membership of the subcommittee, whose names appear on page viii. Their individual expertise and knowledge of transnational operations in the Third World contributed invaluably to refining the immense scope of this statement.

I particularly wish to thank Dr. Isaiah Frank, William L. Clayton Professor of International Economics at The Johns Hopkins University School of Advanced International Studies and director of international economic studies for CED. His excellent work as author of the research study on foreign enterprise in developing countries and as project director for the policy statement deserves special recognition.

Although this policy statement represents only the views of CED's trustees, special gratitude must be extended to the members of CED's counterpart organizations, whose dedication to the initial phase of this project provided a truly international scope to Dr. Frank's research study. The efforts of the following organizations reflect the spirit of friendship, cooperation, and mutual understanding that has characterized our joint projects over many years: the French Institut de l'Entreprise (IDEP), the German European Committee for Economic and Social Progress (CEPES), the British Policy Studies Institute (PSI), the Committee for Economic Development of Australia (CEDA), the Japanese Keizai Doyukai (Japan Committee for Economic Development), and the Swedish Business and Social Research Institute (SNS).

Franklin A. Lindsay, *Chairman*
Research and Policy Committee

CHAPTER ONE

INTRODUCTION
AND
SUMMARY

For the past twenty years, important changes have been taking place in the relationship between U.S. transnational corporations and the countries of the Third World. The volume of direct investment has increased, its origin has become more diversified, and its composition has been shifting. Moreover, in recent years, as each side has shown greater flexibility and a clearer appreciation of the goals and attitudes of the other, strains traditional to the relationship have eased substantially.

Our study of the current status of private direct investment leaves us with the strong conviction that major opportunities now exist for increasing the mutual gains to both transnational corporations and developing nations and, indeed, to the world at large. However, in order for those gains to be realized, it is necessary for each party to understand the other's goals and interests and to adjust its own policies in a spirit of mutual accommodation. Particularly with the prospect of slower growth in the world economy, it is essential to reach such an accommodation so that the dynamic force of the transnational enterprise can make its full contribution to world society, especially to the growth and welfare of the developing countries.

AN EVOLVING RELATIONSHIP

Relations between transnational corporations and developing countries have often been the subject of controversy. As part of the post-World War II drive for political independence and freedom from foreign domination, many developing countries felt the need to consolidate control of their economies by altering the past pattern of relationships with foreign firms. In the resulting adversary atmosphere, extensive government regulations were adopted, and the perceived need to "tame the multinationals" became part of a broader move within the United Nations to create a "new international economic order" that would fundamentally change international rules and institutions governing relations between poor and rich countries.

CHANGING ATTITUDES. Although the rhetoric of dependency and exploitation is still heard at the international political level, changes have taken place in the attitudes of both host governments and transnational corporations that have led to greater mutual understanding and accommodation in their practical, day-to-day relations. Rapidly expanding internal markets and higher levels of knowledge, sophistication, and confidence on the part of government officials have enabled many Third World countries to exert stronger bargaining power in their dealings with foreign companies. At the same time, the companies are more diversified in national origin and type of business and more willing to consider alternatives to the traditional practice of operating through wholly owned subsidiaries. Although host-country fear of foreign domination still exists, it has eased substantially. There is now an appreciation that the relationship with transnationals need not be of the zero-sum variety; rather, it can be one of mutual gain.

RISING INVESTMENT FLOWS. In this improved atmosphere, U.S. direct investment (in constant dollars) in developing countries has doubled in recent years, in comparison with the early 1960s. Moreover, data on financial flows understate the contribution of foreign direct investment because they do not reflect the flow of other resources, such as management, technology, and marketing skills, which may overshadow the contribution of capital.

DIFFERENCES IN PERCEPTION AND OBJECTIVES. Despite greater mutual understanding and an increasing volume of investment, it would be wrong to assume that a convergence of views has been achieved between transnational firms and developing countries on most of the questions that have divided them over the years. Indeed, a wide spectrum of opinions on many issues still exists *within* each group. At the heart of the controversy, a basic difference in perceptions and goals remains. The transnationals, although giving greater recognition to their social responsibilities, still tend to concentrate on the performance of the affiliate, where efficient and profitable operation is regarded as automatically benefiting workers, customers, and suppliers directly and the rest of the host country indirectly through the payment of taxes. Host-government critics, on the other hand, tend to look beyond the internal calculus of the firm and emphasize the perceived broad political, social, and economic effects that the operations of powerful foreign enterprises have on poor countries struggling to achieve not only growth but greater political and economic autonomy and social equity as well.

This fundamental divergence underlies many of the specific issues with which this policy statement is concerned. In this chapter, we summarize our recommendations, which are based on the objective of increasing the gains both to host countries and to transnational enterprises.

THE CLIMATE FOR FOREIGN ENTERPRISE

Most transnationals cite instability in the sense of arbitrary and unpredictable changes in host-government legal, regulatory, and administrative measures as the principal deterrent to operating abroad. As a general principle, we believe that arbitrary actions would be minimized and mutually beneficial relations promoted if changes considered necessary by host countries were made with due regard for the legitimate expectations of transnationals and for the possible impact of these changes on the firms' activities. When governments intervene to promote legitimate social and economic objectives, we recommend that they do so, insofar as possible, by means of measures that work through the market and are reflected in price signals rather than through direct controls.

ACCOMMODATING TO CHANGES IN CIRCUMSTANCES. Foreign firms operate in developing countries under generally applicable laws and regulations and are often also subject to individually negotiated agreements with host governments. As a means of facilitating reasonable and equitable changes in the terms of an agreement, we recommend that consideration be given to including in such agreements procedures for renegotiation in special cases of fundamental, long-term changes in the underlying economic or political environment.

NATIONAL TREATMENT. Although we believe that national policies restricting the access of foreign investment are generally unwise, we do not question the right of host governments to prescribe the fields in which transnational firms may operate. However, with respect to those sectors in which foreign-owned companies *are* permitted to establish affiliates, the basic policy should continue to be treatment no less favorable than that accorded to domestic enterprises, subject to mutually agreed-upon exceptions.

COMPENSATION FOR EXPROPRIATION. It is important that expropriation of the property of transnational corporations be subject not only to due process under host-country laws but also to the internationally accepted standards of prompt, adequate, and effective compensation and to any existing contractual obligations. The determination of equitable compensation can, however, be a complex problem. The best solution may well be to incorporate in the original investment agreement a specific provision that in the event of a dispute regarding compensation, recourse to international arbitration or other previously agreed-upon dispute-settlement facilities may be had at the request of either party.

HOME-GOVERNMENT ROLE. Inasmuch as foreign affiliates of transnationals are subject to the jurisdiction of their host governments, we recommend that home governments play a minimal role in resolving issues that might arise between host governments and transnationals. Nevertheless, it would be unwise to rule out categorically the possibility of employing diplomatic remedies in major disputes when local remedies have been exhausted.

CONFLICTS OF JURISDICTION. Attempts by home countries to impose their own laws and regulations on the foreign affiliates of transnational companies often lead to conflicts of jurisdiction. A good general principle for minimizing such problems is the presumption that where conflicts exist, host-country law takes precedence. However, all jurisdictional issues cannot be resolved by any simple rule; a need therefore exists for bilateral and multilateral agreements that would establish more specific guiding principles and/or provide mutually acceptable procedures for the settlement of such disputes.

VIOLATIONS OF HUMAN RIGHTS. Where questions of host-country violations of human rights arise, no automatic formula can serve as a guide for corporate behavior. Conditions differ from one host country to another; consequently, individual companies will have to apply their own judgments about what is acceptable political behavior when they consider making or expanding investments. However, respect for human rights not only contributes to the long-run health of a society but also can promote a better business environment.

When questions of human rights are at issue, it is important that the U.S. government make its views known to host governments. However, criteria of political morality, when introduced into U.S. government regulations that apply to foreign investments by U.S. firms, may not be effective in a world in which alternative sources of investment are available from countries not subject to U.S. jurisdiction. If it were possible to achieve a reasonable degree of consensus on the part of the major industrial countries, an internationally concerted policy could be applied in individual cases of gross and sustained violations of human rights.

POLITICAL ACTIVITY. Foreign firms should not interfere in the local political process in the sense of resorting to covert activity for the purpose of subverting the political and social system or in the hope of gaining preferential treatment. On the other hand, as a national entity within the host country, there is no reason why a local affiliate of a transnational corporation should not exercise its legitimate political rights openly and fully.

CORRUPT PRACTICES. The definition of legitimate business practice varies from country to country. Regardless of prevailing customs and rules, however, U.S. affiliates should refrain from bribing public officials and from yielding to extortion in order to gain or retain business.* Moreover, we believe it appropriate for the United States, as the largest single source of foreign investment, to take the lead internationally in discouraging such practices through bilateral or multilateral agreements. In particular, we endorse the role of the U.S. government as prime mover behind the efforts of the United Nations Economic and Social Council (ECOSOC) to draft an international agreement barring illicit payments. We also endorse the important self-regulatory activities of the private sector, including those undertaken by the International Chamber of Commerce (ICC), to discourage corrupt practices.

PATTERNS OF COMPANY OPERATION

Although corporate and national goals are not identical, they do not necessarily conflict. Where conflict does exist, it usually reflects the normal divergences between private and public purposes, rather than the fact that a local affiliate is part of a transnational network. It is the task of government to bring private business behavior in line with public purposes by establishing a clear, consistent, and appropriate framework of guidelines and inducements for business to follow.

JOINT VENTURES. As a means of preserving greater local autonomy, developing countries have favored joint ventures over wholly owned subsidiaries and have placed special restrictions on the foreign acquisition of domestic enterprises. Because joint ownership offers potential advantages to both company and host government, we believe that transnationals should not rule out local participants. At the same time, however, it is un-

---

*See memorandum by HENRY B. SCHACHT, page 70.

wise for governments to impose *mandatory* requirements for local equity participation.

TAKEOVERS. We understand and sympathize with the desire of developing countries to nurture and encourage indigenous enterprise. However, we doubt the wisdom of hard-and-fast rules against the foreign acquisition of domestic companies. In some cases, local enterprise may benefit more from the positive effects of innovation and economies of scale as a result of acquisition than from a policy of prohibiting all takeovers. However, when transnationals acquire existing enterprises, we recommend that they consider retaining a substantial local equity interest.

EFFECTS ON LOCAL ENTERPRISE. The takeover issue is part of the developing countries' broader concern with the effects of a foreign firm's entry on the competitive position of local entrepreneurs. Existing firms may be forced out of business, and barriers to the entry of new local entrepreneurs may be created because of the transnational's overwhelming market position. In practice, it is necessary to recognize that the market shares of individual foreign affiliates are often quite modest in particular developing countries. Nevertheless, the abuse of dominant market power is an appropriate subject for public policy regardless of whether the practice in question is engaged in by local affiliates of transnationals or by domestic companies. The remedies may lie primarily in reduction of the shelter from foreign competition enjoyed by local producers as well as in national antitrust regulation.

SEPARATING THE FOREIGN INVESTMENT PACKAGE. *Unbundling* of the foreign investment package—that is, the separating of its components: capital, management, technology, and marketing—is seen by many developing countries as a means of gaining the benefits of foreign resources while maintaining domestic control and increasing the net returns to the host country. Although costs cannot be precisely determined, we doubt that the cost to the host country of the unbundled alternative is generally lower than that of the standard foreign investment package. Nevertheless, a developing country may be willing to pay a price for arrangements that it believes will give it a greater measure of control over its economy.

INDUCEMENTS AND GUARANTEES

TAX CONCESSIONS AND SUBSIDIES. Host countries offer a wide variety of tax and other incentives to attract foreign investment. Transnationals welcome such concessions, but few firms regard them as of more than marginal significance. Far more important are the fundamentals: market opportunities, labor costs and quality, and the economic policies and regulatory environment established by the host government. Developing countries would be well advised, therefore, to be extremely cautious in offering financial and other inducements to foreign investment beyond those specifically intended to compensate for the disincentives inherent in the early stages of development and for host-government policies that discourage inward flows of capital.

SUBSIDIZATION THROUGH PROTECTION.   In order to encourage industrialization and conserve foreign exchange, many Third World countries provide subsidies in the form of a high degree of protection to domestic manufacturing, whether the company is locally or foreign-owned. Although such a policy of *import substitution* does have a legitimate role in a development strategy, it would best advance the host country's interest if it were a rationally designed policy in which the costs of protection were carefully weighed against the gains from stimulating industrialization. In general, a rational policy would provide only *moderate* protection for a *limited* period and would rely mainly on measures such as tariffs, subsidies, and exchange rate policies that preserve the link between domestic and international prices and permit the market to perform its allocation function.

Import-substitution policies are inherently biased against a country's own exports. This bias can be counteracted through measures such as export subsidies. In some cases, however, both import restrictions and export subsidies can be reduced or replaced by the alternative of devaluing the exchange rate.*

REGIONAL ARRANGEMENTS. In many developing countries, the domestic market is too small to allow the economies of scale that are at the basis of industrialization. One escape from this dilemma is regional free-trade arrangements among groups of countries. However, experience does not provide grounds for optimism about the prospect for regional groups. If, despite the difficulties, regional economic integration arrangements could be negotiated and sustained, the broader regional market could provide attractive opportunities for transnational firms to contribute to the industrialization of developing countries.

INTEGRATION INTO THE LOCAL ECONOMY. In various ways, governments of developing countries have attempted to bring about closer integration of foreign operations and the local economy. One method is local-content requirements. Such requirements can help in a strategy of industrialization if they are not so extreme that they impose high costs on the economy and render the final product uncompetitive in world markets. The objective of greater integration into the local economy is also furthered

---

*See memorandum by JACK F. BENNETT, page 70.

through local subcontracting by transnational firms, a practice that we believe should be encouraged.

LOCAL PROCESSING. Third World countries commonly favor policies to promote the local processing of primary materials. However, we do not regard *mandatory* requirements for local processing as being in the long-run interest of these countries. Special measures favoring local processing might be unnecessary if the United States and other industrial countries reduced and ultimately eliminated tariffs and other restrictions on the importation of processed products.

EXPORT TARGETS. Host countries often require transnational corporations to achieve certain export targets that may be unrealistic and cause conflict with the legitimate interests of competing producers in importing countries. The most promising approach in dealing with this problem is twofold: First, it is important that the United States and other industrial countries keep their markets open to exports of those products in which developing countries have acquired or are acquiring a clear comparative advantage. Second, developing countries should try to refrain from export-stimulation practices that go beyond offsetting the distortive effects of other government policies. The recently adopted multilateral subsidy code[1] provides an excellent basis for the practical application of this principle.

HOME-GOVERNMENT INDUCEMENTS. Home-government subsidies for international investment can also lead to undesirable distortions in the flow of capital. We therefore favor an international effort to make incentives and disincentives for foreign investment subject to some sort of multilateral discipline.

Most home countries allow their companies operating abroad to defer payment of taxes on unrepatriated income. For two reasons, we favor continuation of U.S. tax deferral: First, by encouraging the reinvestment of earnings, it contributes to U.S. goals of aiding the development of Third World countries. Second, the absence of deferral would place U.S. firms at a disadvantage in relation to competing firms based in virtually all other home countries.

ROLE OF U.S. OVERSEAS PRIVATE INVESTMENT CORPORATION. The insurance and financing programs of the Overseas Private Investment Corporation (OPIC), which support investment in the Third World, should be reassessed with a view to extending their scope. We appreciate the rea-

---

[1]The code, which limits the use of subsidies affecting foreign trade, is one of the results of the Tokyo Round of Multilateral Trade Negotiations. Virtually all industrial countries are signatories, as are a number of developing countries, including Brazil, India, and Pakistan.

sons for excluding OPIC assistance in the financing of projects to produce commodities and goods for export back to the United States in competition with American production. Such products should not, however, also be subject to special restrictions on access to the U.S. market when they are produced abroad without benefit of unwarranted government incentives or subsidies.

TRANSFER OF TECHNOLOGY

APPROPRIATENESS OF PRODUCTS. Transnationals as well as local firms are guided in what they produce by market demand. To the extent that the resulting pattern of consumption is regarded as excessively sophisticated technologically or socially undesirable, it is up to the host government to discourage such consumption, preferably through taxation applying to all producers, rather than through direct controls or prohibitions.

APPROPRIATENESS OF PRODUCTION PROCESSES. The labor or capital intensity of a country's production processes depends both on the industrial composition of its output and on the particular technology applied to individual industrial operations. We urge developing countries to be extremely cautious in adopting policies (such as concessionary loans for machinery and equipment, overvalued exchange rates that encourage the importation of capital equipment, and restrictions on reducing the labor force when demand slackens) that directly or indirectly promote excessive use of capital-intensive industries or processes.

Both transnational firms and host countries can contribute to the adoption of more appropriate technologies. If companies establish regular procedures for considering technological alternatives, they encourage the cross-fertilization of ideas from different Third World affiliates and stimulate the development of appropriate new technologies. Substantial benefits may also be derived from technological exchanges among labor-abundant developing countries.

PRICE OF TECHNOLOGY. No simple rules can be laid down for the pricing of technology. Clearly, it is to the advantage of a developing country to explore competitive alternatives before negotiating the terms for acquiring technology. In such a negotiation, however, it would be well to bear in mind that the research and development costs of new techniques tend to be high relative to the costs of production of the goods to which they are applied. To attempt to force the transnational corporation down to its marginal cost of supplying the technology may discourage company adaptation, training, and dissemination and may therefore prevent the host country from fully realizing the potential contribution of the technology to its development goals.

RESTRICTIVE CONDITIONS. Host countries are concerned not only about the price of technology but also about the restrictive conditions that may be attached to its use. Companies *not under the common control of a parent firm* should refrain from engaging in practices such as allocating markets or limiting exports. This principle has been incorporated in a set of voluntary guidelines on restrictive business practices recently negotiated by the United States and other countries under the auspices of the United Nations.

RESEARCH AND DEVELOPMENT. A common objective of many developing countries is to reduce their technological dependence on foreign companies. Many transnational affiliates have established local facilities in the Third World for testing products, adapting them to local conditions, controlling quality, and technical trouble-shooting. Serious consideration should be given to the potential of such operations for further development into a local or regional applied-technology center. Where appropriate local institutions already exist, subcontracting of technical services would also be desirable.

EMPLOYMENT OF HOST-COUNTRY NATIONALS. Transnationals generally prefer to employ and train host-country nationals not only for unskilled and skilled manual jobs but for all levels, including technical, financial, and managerial positions. When nonlocal personnel are used, it is frequently because qualified nationals are not available and need to be trained. Arbitrary host-country limits on the use of foreign personnel are therefore generally unnecessary and ill advised.

In order to promote the employment of local managerial and technical personnel, companies provide a wide range of training programs and also make use of existing local or regional management training facilities. We recommend that firms contribute to strengthening such out-company training programs through financial and personnel support.

FINANCIAL ASPECTS OF FOREIGN DIRECT INVESTMENT

The basic effects of the transnational on the host country relate less to the balance of payments than to the company's impact on the country's long-term productive resources and technological capabilities.

BALANCE-OF-PAYMENTS EFFECTS. Developing countries have long been concerned about the balance-of-payments effects of foreign investment. These effects cannot be assessed by simply comparing the inflow of new capital with the outflow of earnings in a given year. Other flows related to the investments, such as changes in imports and exports, must also be taken into account.

BORROWING IN HOST COUNTRIES. Host countries are apprehensive about specific financial implications of transnational operations. For example, companies commonly finance their foreign operations partly by raising funds in the host country as a means of minimizing their foreign exchange risk. The practice has been criticized on the grounds that it reduces the capital contribution of foreign firms to the local economy and that it often deprives local entrepreneurs of their only source of finance. Although these effects are questionable, host countries concerned about the problem have the option, already exercised by some, of setting limits on foreign access to local capital.

PARENT-COMPANY LENDING TO AFFILIATES. In addition to borrowing locally, foreign affiliates may receive loans from their parent companies. Such transactions can constitute a form of local tax avoidance, inasmuch as interest paid on a loan is a deductible expense, whereas profit on equity is taxable. We believe it is legitimate for host countries to regulate intracompany lending, but it is also incumbent on them not to levy excessive taxes on the profits of foreign affiliates.

TRANSFER PRICES. Critics of transnationals contend that transfer prices on intracorporate transactions are often manipulated in order to shift income between jurisdictions, thereby minimizing taxes or circumventing host-country regulations. Transnationals contend, however, that the practice is rarely followed for the purpose of avoiding taxes in developing countries. When special transfer prices are used, they are, rather, intended to ensure that business can earn a reasonable profit where arbitrary limitations are placed on product prices, royalties, administrative charges, and profit remittances.

We endorse the principle included by the Organization for Economic Cooperation and Development (OECD) in its Guidelines for Multinational Enterprises that companies should refrain from manipulating transfer prices for the purpose of avoiding taxes. By the same token, it is important for host countries to refrain from imposing excessive and inequitable taxes on the foreign affiliates.

Many host countries check transfer prices by comparing them with prices for comparable external transactions. Home countries also commonly monitor transfer prices. Collaboration between host and home countries could help to avoid jurisdictional conflicts, especially on the question of allocating joint costs among parts of a transnational enterprise.

INTERNATIONAL ACTION

Because national economic and social objectives differ among sovereign states, the main responsibility for policy on transnational enterprises must continue to reside in host countries and to be reflected in *national* laws, regulations, and practices. Nevertheless, a constructive role can be played by the negotiation of general international standards relating to the operations of transnationals.

CODES OF CONDUCT. The OECD guidelines, adopted in 1976 by the industrial countries, constitute the first set of agreed-upon rules of conduct for transnational corporations applying to countries beyond a strictly regional grouping. Many companies are using the guidelines in formulating their own policies. We urge others to declare their willingness to do so.*

We believe that any U.N. codes relating to transnational enterprise should incorporate the basic principles set forth in the OECD guidelines: voluntary standards rather than legally binding commitments; recognition of the responsibilities of both governments and transnationals; applicability to all international investors, whether private, state-owned, or mixed companies; and inclusion of the principle of respect for international law and national treatment once a foreign enterprise is established.

BILATERAL AGREEMENTS. Bilateral U.S. investment treaties can be an effective means of codifying standards of behavior beyond the lowest common denominator achievable in broad multilateral codes of conduct. We urge the U.S. government to pursue vigorously the negotiation of bilateral investment treaties with developing countries.

STRENGTHENING THE NEGOTIATING CAPACITY OF DEVELOPING COUNTRIES. The United Nations Centre on Transnational Corporations (UNCTC) conducts programs to strengthen the negotiating capacity of developing countries in their dealings with transnational enterprises. We believe it is important that U.S. private business cooperate in these programs by making legal, technical, and financial personnel available for short-term assignments at the Centre to assist in its training and advisory services.* This cooperation could foster mutual understanding of the legitimate aspirations of both parties.

INFORMATION SYSTEMS. Another means of strengthening the bargaining position of developing countries is to improve their knowledge of the operations of transnational corporations.* Information systems for this purpose are being established by two agencies of the United Nations: the Centre on Transnational Corporations and the Industrial Development Organization. Although markets function best when information is fullest,

---

*See memoranda by MARK SHEPHERD, JR., page 70.

many companies have serious doubts about the scope, accuracy, utility, and cost of these systems. It is desirable that the U.S. business community participate more actively in the design and functioning of the systems, so that existing shortcomings can be either corrected or taken into account when the systems are used.

DISPUTE SETTLEMENT. Efforts should be made to include provision for the use of international dispute-settlement facilities in agreements between host governments and transnationals. When such a precaution is taken at the outset, even if it is limited to independent fact-finding, it can help to avoid subsequent costly and disruptive disputes.

CHAPTER TWO

TRANSNATIONAL ENTERPRISE AND THIRD WORLD ECONOMIC DEVELOPMENT:

AN OVERVIEW

In recent years, Third World countries have increased their efforts in the international arena to achieve a fundamental shift in the balance of economic power between rich and poor nations. Despite the well-publicized conflicts, however, there is strong evidence indicating that transnational corporations are becoming more sensitive to the political and social needs of developing countries and that, in general, the Third World is becoming more pragmatic and confident in its dealings with foreign firms.

THE TRANSNATIONAL CORPORATION: WHAT IS IT?

In broad terms, a transnational corporation is a company that operates in several foreign countries through affiliates that are subject to some degree of central control. The parent company's influence may be exercised in a wide variety of ways, including control over such strategic aspects of the affiliate's operations as production and pricing policies, choice of technology, appointment of key personnel, and determination of markets.

The United Nations tends to favor the term *transnational* over *multinational* on the grounds that it is more descriptive of the concept of a parent firm based in one country with operating branches or subsidiaries in a number of foreign countries. In contrast, multinational denotes a company owned by several nationalities, whether or not it has affiliates in other countries. Actually, the preference for transnational is not merely technical; it also rests on the belief that the term more accurately reflects the quality of "domination" inherent in the parent-subsidiary relationship, whereas multinational implies coequality.

CHANGING SCOPE AND TRENDS

Many changes have taken place in the scope and trends of the operations of U.S. transnational enterprises in the Third World. (For a discussion of these changes in more specific quantitative terms, see Appendix B.)

During the past twenty years, U.S. private direct investment in the Third World has increased more rapidly than official development assistance has. Moreover, because of the huge expansion of private bank lending to developing countries, private flows in all forms now greatly exceed the total flow of official resources to the Third World.

Although the United States has lagged behind Germany and Japan in direct investment in the Third World in recent years, just under half the stock of foreign investment in developing countries is still of U.S. origin, with U.S. companies concentrating largely in Latin America. Manufacturing accounts for the largest share of U.S. investment and has been on a rising trend, but investment in petroleum has been on the decline. The most striking increase is in services, much of it reflecting financial operations in offshore centers,[1] such as Bermuda, the Bahamas, and Panama.

From 1978 to 1979, U.S. affiliates in developing countries accounted for just over one-third of income earned from all U.S. foreign direct investment in the form of interest, dividends, and reinvested earnings. Earnings are also received in the form of fees and royalties for technology and management services. Petroleum remains the single largest source of income from investment in the Third World, although its share is diminishing.

ORIGINS OF STRAIN

For many years following World War II, relations between transnational corporations and the countries of the Third World were marked by

---

[1] Offshore financial centers are places that have made a conscious effort to attract nonresident international banking and other financial business denominated in foreign currencies by reducing restrictions on operations and lowering taxes.

strain and conflict. The historical sources of strain in the relationship still color attitudes on both sides despite the very different conditions that prevail today.

After long periods of foreign domination, governments of developing countries, including many that became newly independent after World War II, were determined to consolidate their economic as well as their political control. As part of this process, they sought to break the existing pattern of economic relationships with foreign firms, which they viewed as basically exploitative.

Traditionally concentrated in extractive industries, affiliates of transnational corporations were regarded in much of the Third World as economic enclaves of their home countries, providing only weak backward or forward linkages with the rest of a host-country economy. In the critics' view, transnationals tended to support a pattern of long-term development that would trap poor countries in their poverty because of the inevitable deterioration in the terms of trade for exporters of primary products. At the same time, rich countries would garner an excessive share of the economic rents from foreign operations in the form of both high financial returns to investors and a flow of cheap raw materials for their home-country industries.

Stereotypical views on the role of foreign enterprise in the developing nations also held sway among governments and business groups in the industrial countries, and to some extent, these views persist today. The shortage of capital in the Third World was regarded as the main constraint on development. The role of public capital in the form of bilateral and multilateral economic assistance was conceived as that of helping to finance the social infrastructure (transport, power, communications, and so on) as a precondition for attracting the vast untapped reservoir of private capital in the industrial countries. Against the background of the financial disasters of the 1930s, however, prospects seemed dim in the 1950s and early 1960s for the revival of international capital markets. Private foreign direct investment was therefore regarded as the most promising force for the development of the Third World, providing not only capital but also entrepreneurship, technology, and management. Developing countries were encouraged to provide a "hospitable climate" for foreign investment, including such inducements as tax holidays and subsidies and a minimum of government interference.

The evolving debate became at times a dialogue of the deaf. The transnationals focused on the performance of the firm, maintaining that efficient and profitable operations would automatically bring benefits to the host country in terms of additional workers employed, local taxes paid, and the net contribution of foreign exchange earned or saved. The developing countries went beyond the internal economic calculus of the firm and called attention to perceived broad social and political consequences such as support of reactionary regimes, regressive social pressures, and distortion of traditional cultural values and institutions.

These two sets of stereotypical attitudes were often juxtaposed in international forums in an atmosphere of polarization and confrontation. Particularly within the framework of the United Nations, the desire to "tame the multinationals" became part of a broader drive by the developing nations to effect fundamental changes in international trade and financial relationships by reshaping established rules and institutions to bring about a "new international economic order."

A LESS POLARIZED RELATIONSHIP

Fortunately, the traditional views have been giving way on both sides to a more reasoned and balanced perspective on the problems confronting the Third World and the role of foreign private enterprise in the development process.

Despite continuing rhetoric about dependency and exploitation emanating at the political level, a significant evolution of attitudes has occurred in many developing countries. With increasing diversity in the national origin of foreign direct investment (including the recent emergence of Germany and Japan as major sources), the fear of foreign domination has gradually diminished. With longer contact and experience have come a better understanding of how transnationals operate and an appreciation that the relationship between host country and foreign company need not be of the zero-sum variety but can be one of mutual gain. And with stronger economies and better-trained individuals, many developing countries have acquired greater competence in dealing with transnationals and are more able to shape events and negotiate from positions of greater strength.

At the same time, the companies have reconciled themselves to the reality of dealing with stronger and more assertive host governments in the Third World. In addition, they are also more sensitive to the developing countries' fears of foreign economic domination. The United States itself experienced a wave of concern about domination by the Organization of Petroleum Exporting Countries (OPEC) in the wake of the fourfold oil price increase in 1974 and the massive investment of OPEC financial surpluses in domestic American assets. Numerous proposals were advanced to curb the power of OPEC to "take over" and control the U.S. economy. In the light of this experience, Americans have developed a greater capacity to empathize with the determination of Third World countries to control their own destinies. As a consequence of the changing realities, transnational corporations tend to be more flexible and pragmatic in their approach to the developing countries and have shown a greater willingness to accept some of the constraints on their operations imposed by host governments.

DIVERSITY OF ATTITUDES

In spite of clearly discernible general trends on both sides, attitudes on specific issues are not monolithic. Rather, they tend to reflect the diversity of situations among the developing countries and among transnational firms in different business sectors.

DIVERSITY AMONG DEVELOPING COUNTRIES. Differences in approach to specific foreign direct investment issues are strongly conditioned by the stage of development of the particular country, the nature of its goals and the clarity with which it perceives them, and the sophistication and confidence of the government in dealing with its problems.

The developing countries constitute a much less homogeneous group than the industrial countries do. If we take gross national product per capita as a proxy, however oversimplified, for stage of development, there is a sense in which there is a "North" but no "South." Among the industrial countries of the OECD, the relation between Switzerland, with the highest per capita income, and Ireland, with the lowest, is only about 3 to 1. Among the developing countries, however, even omitting the extremely high-income oil exporters, the relation between per capita income in Singapore and Bangladesh is more than 25 to 1. Conditions and attitudes in some of the high-income developing countries are more similar to those in the industrial countries than to those in the rest of the Third World. Indeed, some of the more successful developing countries are themselves beginning to emerge as home bases for private investment in other Third World countries.[2]

High per capita income and rapid growth in incomes, such as has been experienced in recent years by a number of countries in Latin America and Southeast Asia, tend to increase the bargaining power of host countries in their negotiations with transnationals. They imply not only a rapidly growing domestic market as measured by the growth of total GNP but also an even more quickly expanding demand for the discretionary products in

---

[2]/The greater heterogeneity of the countries of the Third World extends not only to economic conditions but also to political orientation. Although all the OECD countries are representative democracies, the governments of developing nations range from absolute one-man rule to various degrees of broader participation in the political process.

which many transnationals tend to specialize. At the same time, sustained rapid growth may signify the achievement by a country of those qualities of labor, infrastructure, and public and private institutions that attract foreign enterprise to invest in production not only for the home market but for export as well.

Rapid economic growth also increases host-country bargaining power in other ways. Indigenous firms may master the standard technology of established foreign enterprises, undermining the basis for the incentives and priorities accorded them. The attractiveness of an economically dynamic developing country as a market or as an export base may cause transnationals headquartered in different countries, including some based in other Third World nations, to compete for rights of establishment. Options other than the classical foreign direct investment patterns may materialize, including the alternative of acquiring financing and technology through the international banking and consulting networks. Such developments inevitably bring with them alterations in the conditions of regulation, control, and incentives deemed appropriate for transnationals.

Another factor conditioning a developing country's policies is its changing perception of national goals and priorities in the course of its individual development experience. At some stage, for example, a high priority may be placed on the goal of industrialization, pursued initially on the basis of import substitution. This strategy is often characterized by neglect of the agricultural sector and incentives for capital-intensive projects that will adversely affect employment. As the limits of import substitution become apparent, the development strategy may shift to export promotion, greater support for the neglected agricultural sector, and such broad economic and social goals as employment creation and income redistribution. Changing priorities thus lead to shifts in policies toward foreign enterprise as the developing country tries to harness the transnational's operations to the new goals.

Developing-country attitudes are also conditioned by the strength and sophistication of their governments and the confidence with which they deal with problems. The stronger the government, the more consolidated its position, the clearer its objectives, and the better it is able to cope with its problems, the less fear of foreign domination it is likely to have and the more stable its relationships with foreign enterprise—and, indeed, with domestic enterprise—are likely to be.

DIVERSITY AMONG TRANSNATIONALS. The position of transnationals should also be viewed in differentiated terms. The bargaining relationships of transnationals with host governments are likely to differ for the various models of foreign investment: natural resource projects, manufacturing investments to serve the local market, manufacturing investments primarily for export, and service industries. Typically (but not always), host-country leverage will be strongest in the first two cases. Corporations are frequently willing to accept highly restrictive conditions in exchange for the exclusive right to develop and mine a rich ore deposit or to manufacture locally for a large, rapidly growing, and often protected domestic market. However, they are likely to be less willing to make such concessions in order to site their manufacturing for export in a particular developing country because acceptable alternative export bases are generally available. In the case of service industries, it is impossible to generalize because of the wide variety of fields in which they operate.

Transnationals are also subject to different time profiles in their bargaining relationships with host countries depending on the industrial sector in which they operate. In the case of a natural resource venture, the leverage of the host country will tend to strengthen over time because of the large front-end commitment the transnational enterprise must make. Similarly, a manufacturing firm using standardized technology to produce conventional goods may find that its bargaining position erodes over time as local entrepreneurs and labor acquire the skills to operate on their own. In contrast, a high-technology manufacturing company is likely to maintain its bargaining power because its contribution to the host country's economy depends on a continuing flow of resources from the parent firm in the form of new technology applying to both processes and products.

EVALUATING THE TRANSNATIONAL CONTRIBUTION

What has been the impact of transnational corporations on development in the Third World?

The essence of the case for foreign investment (and, presumably, the reason most developing countries try to attract it) is that it brings with it a package of resources which adds to the output and real income of the host country an amount greater than that accruing to the investor in the form of profits and interest. The increase in income that does not go to the investor must accrue to other groups. It may benefit labor in the form of higher real wages and more employment, consumers through lower prices and a wider choice of better-quality products, and the host government in the form of higher tax revenues that can be spent on behalf of the society as a whole.

If foreign investment results in material gains not only to the investor but also to these various local beneficiaries, why has there been so much controversy over the impact of transnationals on economic development?

So long as the investment meets the market test of profitability, is it not obvious that it cannot be a zero-sum game but must be one of mutual benefit to foreign enterprise and host country? Unfortunately, these questions cannot be answered unequivocally because of considerations relating to externalities, distortions, attribution, and alternatives.

EXTERNALITIES. Some of the most important effects of foreign investment are not reflected in calculations based on market-determined costs of inputs and prices of outputs. Positive external benefits include stimulating indigenous entrepreneurship through local subcontracting or demonstration effects, inducing an expansion of production in other sectors of the economy in which capacity is underutilized, imparting new skills to workers who may later be hired by local companies, introducing new technology that may find uses elsewhere in the economy and lead to lower costs and better products, and contributing to a more efficient local market structure by exerting competitive pressure on the insulated position of a local monopolist.

Although there may be benefits, there may also be certain social costs: stifling of newly emerging entrepreneurs who cannot match the superior technical, financial, and managerial resources of a transnational corporation; depriving indigenous firms of their main source of capital because of local borrowing by transnationals; introducing highly capital-intensive technology in the face of widespread underemployment of local labor; driving out existing local competition and establishing a dominant position in the host market; and exacerbating local inequalities by locating production facilities in the most developed regions of the host country.

DISTORTIONS. Difficulties of evaluation also arise because the private firm's accounting may itself be distorted by actions taken by the host government. If a firm produces for the host-country market, the value of its output may be exaggerated by artificially high prices for its products as a result of tariffs or other government restrictions on imports of comparable products. At the same time, imported equipment, components, and materials may be obtained at artificially low prices because of an overvalued exchange rate maintained by the government through a system of exchange controls. Similarly, direct government subsidies, tax holidays, and other incentives may result in costs of inputs and prices of outputs that deviate from their actual social accounting prices based on relative scarcity.

The situation or policies of the transnational itself may cause distortions. The firm may possess some unique advantage, such as special technology or a trademark, that permits it to charge a higher price for its products than would prevail in a more competitive market. Or it may, for tax or other reasons, set arbitrary transfer prices on its intracorporate transactions.

In evaluating the contribution of foreign investment to development, corrections need to be made for both externalities and distortions. This process consists of assigning "shadow prices" in place of actual prices. Shadow pricing involves ascribing values that correspond more closely than market prices do to the real social costs of inputs and the real social benefits of outputs. This technique is highly imprecise. However, it is perhaps less subject to serious error when applied to distortions than when applied to externalities because of the greater likelihood, in the case of distortions, of the existence of price data that reflect the realities of economic scarcity.

ATTRIBUTION. At the base of much of the controversy surrounding the evaluation of the role of foreign enterprise in developing countries lies the confusion arising from mistaken attribution. This difficulty can best be conveyed through examples: If a country's overvalued exchange rate encourages a firm to import more machinery and employ less labor than it otherwise would, is the firm to be blamed, or is the problem one of government policy? Or suppose that a foreign enterprise locates a new plant in the capital of a country because of the attraction of an ample supply of skilled labor, transportation, and other infrastructure. Is its neglect of the more critical social need for new investment in the country's more backward regions related to the "foreignness" or "transnationality" of the firm, or is it a reflection of the normal decision-making process that takes place in any private firm, whether domestic or foreign? Does the remedy lie in some special government action directed at foreign companies or in more general government incentives or disincentives designed to adjust private investment decision making into line with broader social objectives?

ALTERNATIVES. Logically, any assessment of the net affects of foreign investment should specify the alternatives with which it is being compared. In the case of a foreign investment to produce for the local market, the host country presumably has a number of choices: It can import the product. Or a local firm might raise the capital and other resources domestically and set up a plant. Or the capital might be borrowed abroad and the technology and management hired through a licensing agreement. Or a joint venture might be set up involving the mobilization of resources both in the host country and from abroad.

With the exception of importing, however, these theoretical alternatives may not always be available. Although capital might be independently borrowed, know-how in a particular case might not be obtainable except through direct investment by a foreign firm. A precise and detailed consideration of available alternatives, therefore, cannot take place at a macroeconomic level; it is possible only at the level of individual project evaluation.

In sum, it is apparent that major difficulties and uncertainties surround any effort to evaluate the impact of foreign investment on developing countries. In the long run, the most fundamental consideration may be, not the current transnational contribution to the production and income of host countries, but the extent to which the operations of transnationals enable developing countries to absorb the skills and techniques that strengthen their own capabilities for sustained industrial growth.

MAXIMIZING THE GAINS

Both developing countries and transnational corporations are increasingly aware that the impact of foreign enterprise on development is not a subject for broad generalization. Because foreign investment can have a spectrum of effects, and because many of those effects are so difficult to quantify, the most practical contribution is to try to design realistic policies to maximize beneficial effects over the detrimental consequences.

The tools in the hands of a host country for attempting to maximize the contribution of transnational firms to its development goals (apart from its success in managing its economy generally) are direct regulation and the use of market incentives and disincentives. How these tools are deployed depends on the nature of the foreign investment and the relative bargaining power of the parties to the negotiation.

But bargaining is a subtle process. Over time, the total investment gains to be distributed to host country and transnational are unlikely to be independent of how these gains are divided. A better mutual understanding of each other's interests and attitudes should lead to more enlightened policies that may expand the total gains and increase the absolute returns to both sides. Moreover, although host countries and transnationals are the principal parties in this relationship, the roles of home governments and international organizations must also be considered.

CHAPTER THREE

THE CLIMATE FOR
FOREIGN INVESTMENT

Two basic facts underlie the foreign investment relationship: First, all countries have the right to limit the establishment of transnational corporations and to regulate their operations. Second, transnationals cannot be forced to invest in a country; they must be attracted.

The decision of a firm to establish a presence in a particular host country will, of course, be affected in the first instance by the usual economic and financial considerations that enter into any investment decision. When considering an investment abroad, however, a corporation will give special attention to the investment environment in the country and the likelihood that it will remain reasonably stable over the life of the investment.

LAW AND REGULATION

An acceptable investment climate need not imply an ideological orientation in favor of a free enterprise system along the lines familiar to the West. Indeed, stable and mutually profitable arrangements, including joint ventures and technology-sale agreements, have been established between transnational firms and the Socialist countries of Eastern Europe. With their strong governments and clear sense of national purpose, these countries have, by and large, been able to offer the companies firm and well-defined conditions without fear of being dominated by a foreign presence.

Many developing countries operate to a considerable extent through state enterprises where market principles may not govern economic behavior. As in the case of the Socialist countries, a nonmarket orientation need not be an absolute deterrent to a productive role for foreign private enterprise.

Transnationals point to *instability* as the principal deterrent to investing and operating in the Third World. By instability they do not necessarily mean political upheavals accompanied by changes in regime. Although such crises cause foreign investment to fall off temporarily, it tends to recover as a new regime consolidates its position.

More important are forms of instability that do not necessarily result from internal political upheavals. These include threats of political action; abrupt changes in conditions of operation such as ownership and remittance regulations; complex, drawn-out, and arbitrary bureaucratic procedures; and more generally, the prospect of unpredictable alterations in the rules of the game after investment decisions have been made and resources committed to the foreign operation.

LIVING WITH INSTABILITY. Companies generally recognize that changes in host-government policies are inevitable as Third World countries undergo the profound social and economic transformation that constitutes development. Moreover, they have come to accept and live with changes in policies, both at home and abroad, that reflect legitimate responses to altered conditions. Nevertheless, they perceive the degree of instability of laws and regulations and the arbitrariness of administrative practices as especially acute in many developing countries.

Given the reality of changing circumstances and priorities in developing countries, what can be done to foster greater clarity and stability in the conditions under which transnationals must operate? As a general principle, when host countries consider changes necessary in the framework of national law and regulation affecting the operation of transnationals, arbitrary actions would be minimized and mutually beneficial relations promoted if those changes are made with due regard to the legitimate expectations of transnational corporations and the impact of the changes on their activities.

Foreign affiliates in developing countries not only operate under generally applicable national laws and regulations but also are often subject to individually negotiated agreements with host governments. However, the host countries may feel that long-standing agreements are vestiges of neocolonial relationships, that they reflect unequal bargaining power and negotiating skills, or simply that fundamental changes have taken place in domestic or world market conditions. Under such circumstances, governments may seek to reopen the terms of a contract with a foreign business.

Many transnational firms appreciate that over time conditions may alter the equity of a contract with a host government and that as a practical matter it is difficult for lopsided agreements to survive. Moreover, the firms may at times find that it is in their interest to seek contractual revisions. **As a means of facilitating reasonable and equitable changes in the terms of a contract, we recommend that consideration be given to including at the outset procedures for renegotiation in special cases of fundamental, long-term changes in the underlying economic or political environment.**

TYPES OF GOVERNMENT INTERVENTION

The climate for foreign investment is affected by the ways in which governments intervene in the economy to advance their national goals. Broadly speaking, governments can seek to alter the play of market forces by either of two means: suspending the operation of the market through prohibitions, mandated requirements, and direct controls or working through the market to alter its incentives by means of taxes and subsidies. For example, if a government decides to protect a particular industry from import competition, it can do so either by levying a tariff or by imposing an import quota. In terms of economic efficiency, the tariff has the advantage of preserving the link between domestic and world prices, whereas the quota breaks that link completely.

Apart from their disadvantage in reducing the effectiveness of price signals as an allocator of resources, direct controls produce side effects on the investment climate that are likely to be especially adverse in the context of conditions widely prevalent in developing countries. Controls require much more administration than interventions that work through the market. If an import quota is imposed, someone must decide who gets the licenses to import. The substitution of administrative decision for the market as an allocator of scarce imports can place an enormous burden on precisely those types of administrative skills that are typically in short supply in developing countries. Moreover, the temptation to corruption is great when low-income civil servants have to make decisions about the allocation of import licenses that may have great value to the recipients.

It is probably no exaggeration that the single most important cause of bureaucratic delays, arbitrary decisions, and widespread corruption in developing countries is excessive reliance on direct controls. **We recommend, therefore, that when governments intervene in economic activity**

to promote legitimate social and economic objectives, they do so insofar as possible through measures that work through the market and are reflected in price signals rather than through direct controls. Such a policy would go a long way toward improving the climate not only for foreign companies but for domestic enterprise as well.[1]

NATIONAL TREATMENT AND EXPROPRIATION. As stated at the beginning of this chapter, governments have the right to prescribe the fields in which transnational firms may operate. For reasons of public order or national security, most governments prohibit foreign enterprise in such activities as communications, electric power generation and distribution, and defense industries. **However, in those business sectors where transnationals have the right of establishment, the basic host-country policy should continue to be treatment under national laws, regulations, and administrative practices that is no less favorable than that accorded to domestic enterprises, subject to mutually agreed-upon exceptions.**

We recognize the sovereign right of all states to nationalize private property. However, **in the event of expropriation of the property of transnational corporations, it is important that such action be subject not only to due process under the laws of the host country but also to the internationally accepted standard of prompt, adequate, and effective compensation and to any contractual obligations to which the host government has subscribed.**

These principles of national treatment and appropriate compensation in the event of expropriation can contribute significantly to an improved investment climate, particularly if they are formally included both in the laws of host countries and in the treaties between host and home governments.

No formal provisions, however, can fully protect a company against arbitrary and inequitable actions. A determined government can achieve de facto nationalization while avoiding outright expropriation. Without violating the letter of any law or agreement, a government can cripple an enterprise through measures such as unreasonable price controls, profit limitations, or confiscatory taxes. The result is "creeping expropriation."

Even with the best intentions, the determination of equitable compensation in the case of nationalization can be a complex problem. Restitution based on simple definitions such as net book value fail to compensate a company for lost profit opportunities or investments in intangible assets such as goodwill and marketing efforts. Other formulas based on the capi-

---

[1] For an illuminating discussion of types of state intervention in developing economies, see V. N. Balasubramanyam, "The Economic Framework of Development" (Paper presented at the Abidjan Conference of the International Chamber of Commerce, October 29–31, 1979, Abidjan, Ivory Coast).

talization of earning capacity also have limitations. **The best method for resolving disputes over compensation for nationalized property may well be to incorporate in the original investment agreement a specific provision that, in such cases, recourse to international arbitration or other previously agreed-upon dispute-settlement facilities may be had at the request of either party.**

JURISDICTION. Transnational corporations recognize that their foreign affiliates are subject to the jurisdiction of the countries in which they operate. Normally, disputes between a state and a transnational that are not amicably settled between the parties are subject to the jurisdiction of the courts of that state. Exceptions are cases in which the state agrees to third-party settlement, an arrangement that we believe is desirable for resolving disputes on such major issues as compensation for nationalized property.

A number of host countries, especially in Latin America, have written into their foreign investment law the principle known as the *Calvo Clause,* named after the Argentine minister who first propounded it. Under this doctrine, foreign subsidiaries of transnational corporations are expected to give up access to diplomatic support from the government of the parent company in case of disputes between the foreign investor and the host government and to seek remedies entirely within local law and the local judicial system.

The presumption underlying the Calvo Doctrine is that the authority of the host government will be applied to both local and foreign enterprise on a nondiscriminatory basis. In part because this assumption of nondiscrimination has been questioned, the U.S. government has sought not only "national treatment" for its investors abroad but also assurances of "equitable" treatment.

On the question of diplomatic support from the governments of parent companies, **we recommend that home governments play a minimal role in issues between host governments and transnationals. Nevertheless, it would be unwise to rule out categorically the possibility of diplomatic representation in the case of major disputes in which local remedies have been exhausted.**

Another type of jurisdictional problem arises from home-country attempts to project their own laws and regulations onto foreign affiliates. American transnationals believe that the extraterritorial reach of U.S. antitrust legislation not only may conflict with host-country law but also places them at a disadvantage relative to competitive firms based in other industrial countries not subject to such extraterritoriality. U.S. companies have also been caught in the middle of conflicts of jurisdiction with respect to home-country regulations such as capital controls, restrictions on trade with Communist countries, antiboycott legislation, and transfer-pricing rules. In the latter case, for example, home-country tax authorities may insist that parent companies charge a royalty for technology, but the host country may forbid the subsidiary to pay it.

Although most U.S. companies operating abroad have experienced conflicts of jurisdiction, few regard these as among their most serious problems. Nevertheless, **a good general principle for minimizing jurisdictional problems between home and host countries would be a presumption that where conflicts exist, host-country law takes precedence. However, because all jurisdictional issues cannot be resolved by any simple rule, bilateral or multilateral agreements between home and host countries are needed to establish more specific jurisdictional principles and/or provide mutually acceptable procedures for the settlement of conflicts.**

THE FOREIGN POLITICAL CONTEXT

How should U.S. transnationals respond to host-country political and social conditions and practices that may diverge sharply from the norms to which the firms are accustomed in their home countries?

OBJECTIONABLE SOCIAL AND POLITICAL CONDITIONS. No simple formula can serve as a guide for corporate behavior in countries in which questions of human rights violations arise. Because conditions differ from host country to host country, each company will have to use its own judgment about acceptable political behavior when it considers making or expanding investments. Respect for human rights not only contributes to the long-run health of a society but can also promote a better business environment.

To the extent that repression and other serious violations of human rights reflect political instability, companies are generally concerned with their impact on business risk and performance. Company attitudes are also conditioned by stockholder reaction and, more broadly, by public opinion. At the extreme, brutality and oppression by a particular country can become so morally repugnant that investing in that country would in all probability be out of the question.

Third World countries often regard human rights as comprising not only political elements but, equally important, the social and economic circumstances under which people live and work. In many cases, deplorable conditions simply reflect a country's poverty. In other cases, such conditions reflect or are accentuated by policies of discrimination against particular racial, religious, or other groups. Some firms take the position that they are helping to ameliorate such situations by working within the system; they provide not only jobs for the disadvantaged groups but also benefits such as training facilities, housing, and health clinics.

In contrast with actions by individual firms, companies regard U.S. government policies and regulations to promote human rights in foreign countries with strong skepticism. Many express the view that home-government trade and investment policies are neither appropriate nor effective instruments for this purpose. They stress the ambiguity of the standards of acceptable social and political behavior and the severe obstacles encountered in response to U.S. government efforts to apply consistent policies in widely disparate situations.

When questions of human rights are at issue, it is important that the U.S. government make its views known to host governments. However, criteria of political morality, when introduced into U.S. government regulations that apply to foreign investments of U.S. firms, may not be effective in a world in which alternative sources of investment are available from companies not subject to U.S. jurisdiction. If it were possible to achieve a reasonable degree of consensus on the part of the major industrial countries, an internationally concerted policy could be applied in individual cases of gross and sustained violations of human rights.

INVOLVEMENT IN LOCAL POLITICS. It is sometimes asserted as a principle of good corporate behavior that transnationals should not interfere in the internal political affairs of the foreign countries in which they operate. Whether this proposition has merit depends on what is meant by *interfere*.

Foreign firms should not interfere in the local political process in the sense of resorting to covert activity for the purpose of subverting the political and social system or in the hope of gaining preferential treatment. On the other hand, as a national entity within the host country, there is no reason why a local affiliate of a transnational corporation should not exercise its legitimate political rights openly and fully. To refrain from doing so would be especially anomalous as affiliates increasingly take the form of joint ventures with local interests.

CORRUPT PRACTICES. The definition of legitimate business practices varies from country to country. For example, business contributions of money or services to a political organization are accepted practice in some countries, frowned on in others, and illegal in still others. **Regardless of prevailing customs and rules, however, it is important that U.S. affiliates refrain from bribing public officials and from yielding to extortion.***

The United States has made a major effort to discourage corrupt practices abroad. Under the Foreign Corrupt Practices Act of 1977, American

---

*See memorandum by HENRY B. SCHACHT, page 70.

corporations are prohibited from bribing a foreign government official for the purpose of obtaining preferential treatment.

U.S. companies have expressed concern that the lack of similar legislation in other major industrial countries could place them at a competitive disadvantage. Fears have also been voiced about ambiguities in the law and in its administration that inhibit U.S. corporate investment and operations abroad. Among the principal issues are disclosure requirements, the extent to which U.S. companies are held accountable for the acts of their foreign subsidiaries and agents, and the interpretation of the exemption for "facilitating payments." **We believe legislative action to clarify ambiguities in the Foreign Corrupt Practices Act would be desirable.**

Some companies believe that regulating corrupt practices is not a job for the home country but should be left to the host government. They regard as patronizing such attempts by home countries to export their own standards of business morality.

While recognizing these problems, **we believe it appropriate for the United States, as the largest single source of foreign investment, to take the lead in discouraging foreign corrupt practices through bilateral or multilateral agreements.* In particular, we endorse the role of the U.S. government as prime mover behind the efforts of the United Nations Economic and Social Council to draft an international agreement barring illicit payments.** An international code would also help to eliminate the competitive disadvantages under which some U.S. companies operate.

We endorse the important self-regulatory activities of the private sector in discouraging corrupt practices. Many American companies have drawn up individual corporate codes of conduct establishing guidelines for international transactions. They have also played a prominent role in the development of the voluntary code of ethical practices for transnational corporations adopted by the International Chamber of Commerce.

---

*See memorandum by HENRY B. SCHACHT, page 71.

CHAPTER FOUR

PATTERNS
OF COMPANY
OPERATION

Most developing countries find themselves caught in a dilemma. On the one hand, they appreciate the contribution that transnational corporations can make toward the realization of their national economic goals and even go so far as to offer special inducements to attract foreign enterprise. On the other hand, they are concerned about the loss of local autonomy implied by foreign ownership and control of major sectors of the domestic economy. This problem is regarded as especially serious in small countries with highly concentrated production structures and in countries, regardless of size, with relatively weak political systems and poor economic management.

Among their specific concerns in this context are the relationship between national and corporate goals, the competitive effects on local entrepreneurs of the superior performance of foreign affiliates, and the restrictions imposed by the parent company on the entrepreneurial freedom accorded such affiliates. As a means of preserving a greater measure of local control, developing countries have favored joint ventures with a substantial local interest over wholly owned subsidiaries and have placed special restrictions on the foreign acquisition of existing enterprises. In addition, a number of Third World nations have called for the unbundling of the foreign investment package, especially in basic resource industries.

NATIONAL AND CORPORATE GOALS

Affiliates of foreign firms commonly pursue such company goals as profit optimization, diversification of raw material sources, preempting or maintaining a foreign market position, and attaining some rate of overall growth in sales or earnings.

The national goals of the host country, on the other hand, emphasize public objectives. These include maximization of tax revenues and employment, export stimulation, the development of a local technological and entrepreneurial capacity, encouragement of small industries, rural development, improvement in income distribution, development of neglected regions, and other broad social and economic objectives.

We recognize that corporate and national goals are not identical. However, the fact that they are different does not imply that they are necessarily conflicting. On the contrary, many of the goals of transnationals are fully compatible with those of the developing nations in which they operate. Where conflict does exist, it usually reflects the normal differences between private and public purposes and may have little to do with the fact that a local affiliate is part of a transnational network. **We believe that it is the task of government to bring private business behavior into line with public purposes by establishing an appropriate framework of laws, regulations, and incentives.** This role of government is understood and accepted by business firms at home, and there is no reason to question its legitimacy when operating abroad.

JOINT VENTURES

Transnational enterprises have traditionally preferred to establish wholly owned subsidiaries, especially when operating in Third World countries. However, marked differences in the trends of ownership patterns exist among corporations based in different home countries.

As the data in Table 1 indicate, most affiliates of U.S.-based companies are wholly owned. Although this predominance has persisted since the early 1950s, a clear trend toward an increasing proportion of minority-owned U.S. affiliates is discernible. In the case of European-based affiliates, minority ownership has become the most common form, accounting for more than 40 percent of all newly established affiliates from 1966 to 1970.

The most striking trend toward minority ownership, however, is among Japanese-based affiliates; the proportion has grown from 16 percent before 1951 to 74 percent in the 1966-to-1970 period. Most Japanese investment took place in the latter part of these two decades. As comparative late-

TABLE 1

**Distribution of Ownership Patterns[a] of 1,276 Manufacturing Affiliates[b]
of 391 Transnational Corporations Established
in Developing Countries, by Period of Establishment, 1951 to 1975**

Home Country and Type and Ownership	Number Established as Percentage of Total				
	Before 1951	1951–1960	1961–1965	1966–1970	1971–1975
Affiliates of 180 U.S.-based corporations					
Total	**100.0**	**100.0**	**100.0**	**100.0**	**100.0**
Wholly owned	**58.4**	**44.5**	**37.4**	**46.2**	**43.7**
Majority owned	**12.2**	**21.4**	**19.2**	**17.8**	**17.3**
Co-owned	**5.6**	**7.9**	**11.4**	**11.2**	**10.4**
Minority owned	**11.2**	**18.8**	**21.7**	**21.5**	**28.1**
Unknown	**12.6**	**7.4**	**10.3**	**3.3**	**0.4**
Affiliates of 135 European- and U.K.-based corporations					
Total	**100.0**	**100.0**	**100.0**	**100.0**	—
Wholly owned	**39.1**	**31.6**	**20.9**	**18.9**	—
Majority owned	**15.4**	**20.1**	**15.6**	**16.4**	—
Co-owned	**5.3**	**6.6**	**11.1**	**6.6**	—
Minority owned	**9.8**	**27.9**	**35.8**	**42.1**	—
Unknown	**30.5**	**13.9**	**16.6**	**16.0**	—
Affiliates of 76 other transnational corporations[c]					
Total	**100.0**	**100.0**	**100.0**	**100.0**	—
Wholly owned	**27.4**	**16.7**	**10.7**	**6.1**	—
Majority owned	**8.2**	**26.2**	**12.6**	**8.2**	—
Co-owned	**12.3**	**7.1**	**6.3**	**7.5**	—
Minority owned	**16.4**	**42.9**	**66.7**	**74.2**	—
Unknown	**35.6**	**7.1**	**3.8**	**3.9**	—

[a]Affiliates of which the parent firm of the system owns 95 percent or more are classified as wholly owned; over 50 percent, as majority owned; equal percentages as co-owned; 5 to under 50 percent, as minority owned.

[b]The affiliates of U.S.-based corporations are those in which the U.S.-based parent of a transnational enterprise held a direct equity interest; the affiliates of corporations based in the United Kingdom, Western Europe, and Japan include those in which parent companies held equity interest indirectly through other affiliates.

[c]Of these 76 corporations, 61 are based in Japan.

Note: Due to rounding, percent totals may not equal 100.

SOURCE: United Nations, *Transnational Corporations in World Development: A Reexamination* (New York: United Nations, 1978), p. 229, based on data supplied by the Harvard Multinational Enterprise Project.

comers in establishing foreign affiliates, the Japanese have undoubtedly faced greater host-country pressure to enter into joint ventures. Other contributing factors are the heavy Japanese concentration in extractive industries, an area in which developing countries often insist on domestic majority ownership, and the sensitivity of the Japanese to their postwar image in the formerly occupied areas of eastern and southern Asia.

Companies that favor wholly owned operations in the Third World offer a variety of reasons for their preference; the most important is the desire to maintain centralized management and decision making for the parent system. Other reasons include the desire to avoid the dilution of equity returns, ensuring greater security for technological know-how, and concern about pressure from domestic shareholders for quick returns in the form of dividends when the firm might prefer to reinvest local earnings.

Joint ownership is more acceptable to transnationals if they can maintain management control and if potential local partners are established and responsible business firms. It may increase the firm's identification with the domestic economy and reduce the inevitable onus of being a foreign company.

From the host-country point of view, joint ventures are a means of diluting foreign control of important segments of the host economy. They may also be a vehicle for facilitating the acquisition of the technology, skills, and other capabilities of the transnational. More generally, the desire for local participation presumes a greater responsiveness to national goals on the part of domestic owners compared to foreign investors. It is an open question, however, whether local partners would necessarily be more responsive than foreign owners, who often make a special and conscious effort to be seen as good corporate citizens when operating abroad.

Given the potential advantages to both sides, we believe that transnational corporations should not rule out local participants. At the same time, however, it is unwise for governments to impose *mandatory* requirements for local equity participation. Because of their proprietary knowledge and strong bargaining positions, high-technology industries in particular may be deterred from entry by such requirements, thereby depriving the developing country of the benefit of investment by some of the most innovative and dynamic enterprises.

TAKEOVERS

More than a third of the subsidiaries of U.S. transnationals in developing countries have been established through the acquisition of going concerns (Table 2). Developing countries tend to look with disfavor on such

TABLE 2

Foreign Manufacturing Subsidiaries of 376 Multinational Enterprises, Classified by Whether Newly Formed or Acquired as Going Concerns[a]

Location and Classification	Subsidiaries of 180 U.S.-based Enterprises		Subsidiaries of 135 Europe- and U.K.-based Enterprises		Subsidiaries of 61 Japan-based Enterprises		Subsidiaries of All 376 Enterprises in Sample	
	Number	Percent	Number	Percent	Number	Percent	Number	Percent
In Industrialized Countries								
Total subsidiaries	**3,603**	**100.0**	**3,207**	**100.0**	**46**	**100.0**	**6,856**	**100.0**
Acquired as going concerns	1,974	54.8	1,705	53.1	8	17.4	3,687	53.8
Newly formed	1,385	38.4	862	26.9	38	82.6	2,285	33.3
Other and unknown	244	6.8	640	20.0	0	0	884	12.9
In Developing Countries								
Total subsidiaries	**2,124**	**100.0**	**1,454**	**100.0**	**516**	**100.0**	**4,094**	**100.0**
Acquired as going concerns	757	35.6	465	32.0	72	14.0	1,294	31.6
Newly formed	1,224	57.6	715	49.2	433	83.9	2,372	57.9
Other and unknown	143	6.7	274	18.8	11	2.1	428	10.5

aData for U.S.-based enterprises are provisional as of 1975; others are final as of 1970.

Note: Due to rounding, percent totals may not equal 100.

SOURCE: Raymond Vernon, *Storm Over the Multinationals* (Cambridge, Mass.: Harvard University Press, 1977), p. 72, based on data in the Harvard Multinational Enterprise Project.

acquisitions, regarding them as alienating the domestic economy without providing offsetting benefits. In some cases, takeovers are seen as intended to reduce competition and increase the dominant position of the foreign affiliate.

The fact is, however, that foreign firms rarely acquire an existing local company for the purpose of simply continuing its operations as before. New products may be introduced; old equipment may be overhauled. A transnational may combine some special capability in design, engineering, or production with the local company's knowledge and skill in distribution in the local market. With greater efficiency, prices may go down rather than up.

We understand and sympathize with the desire of developing countries to nurture and encourage the growth of indigenous enterprise, but we doubt the wisdom of hard-and-fast rules against foreign acquisitions as a means of advancing that objective. In some cases, local enterprise may benefit more in the long run from the positive effects of technological and organizational innovation and economies of scale as a result of acquisitions than from the policy of prohibiting all takeovers. **When transnationals acquire existing local enterprises, we recommend that consideration be given to retaining a substantial local equity interest in the acquired company.**

EFFECTS ON LOCAL ENTREPRENEURS

The takeover issue is part of the broader host-country concern with the effects of the entry of a foreign firm on existing or potential local firms in the same business. The fear is that the indigenous entrepreneurs will be smothered when transnationals, with their tremendous technological and financial resources, establish affiliates in developing countries. Not only may existing firms be forced out of business, but barriers may be created to the entry of new, local entrepreneurs because of the transnationals' advertising, promotion, and product-differentiation practices, bolstered by established brand names and trademarks.

Here, too, generalizations are of questionable value. In the extractive and high-technology manufacturing sectors, existing or potential local competition is usually from other foreign enterprises rather than from indigenous firms. But active competition from indigenous firms is not uncommon in such manufacturing fields as food processing, textiles, and other consumer product sectors. Often, however, the domestic and foreign firms cater to different segments of the market. Moreover, the presence of the foreign firm generally stimulates local entrepreneurship through the upgrading of local products, the expansion of local markets, and subcontracting to local suppliers.

It is possible that particular firms may, through some special advantage, be in a position to abuse a dominant market position. In practice, however, the market shares of individual foreign affiliates are often quite modest in particular developing countries. *Nevertheless, the abuse of market power is an appropriate subject for public policy, regardless of whether the practice in question is engaged in by local affiliates of transnationals or by domestic companies. The remedies may lie primarily in the reduction or elimination of the shelter from foreign competition enjoyed by local producers as well as in national antitrust regulation.*

UNBUNDLING THE FOREIGN INVESTMENT PACKAGE

The distinctive characteristic of the traditional pattern of foreign investment is its combination in a single package of a variety of resources: capital, management, technology, and marketing. Many developing countries see the unbundling of this package as a means of retaining control of important sectors of the domestic economy and increasing the net returns to the host country from the use of foreign resources. Japan is often cited as an example of a country that has historically resisted direct foreign investment while successfully industrializing on the basis of foreign technology and other resources acquired for a fee.

Unbundling has progressed farthest in the petroleum field, where it has become, in one form or another, the rule rather than the exception. Among the types that have been adopted, particularly in petroleum, are service contracts, production-sharing agreements, and technical assistance agreements. In some cases, the foreign enterprise assumes most of the front-end risk as well as the major management responsibility. However, despite the new emphasis on the state as owner and the transnational as contractor, the difference between such arrangements and the traditional concession agreement is largely formal.

Outside the petroleum field, high-technology firms have demonstrated the least willingness to unbundle. Firms outside the high-technology field are willing to respond, although with differing degrees of enthusiasm, to a developing country's desire to unbundle the foreign investment package provided prospective returns and risks are reasonable. Unless the foreign firm can retain control of the operation, however, it is unlikely to permit use of its brand names or trademarks, which are identified with certain standards of quality.

Virtually all firms participating in our interview study expressed the view that the cost to the host country of acquiring financial, technical, managerial, and marketing resources through unbundling is substantially greater than that of the standard foreign investment package. Nevertheless, a developing country may be willing to pay a price for what it regards as a more satisfactory arrangement in terms of its objective of gaining a greater measure of control of its economy.

As the number of transnational corporations of diverse types and nationalities increases, host-country options for acquiring foreign resources are expanding. Whether service contracts and other forms of unbundled arrangements can be sufficiently attractive will, of course, depend on the details of the bargains struck in particular cases. In the increasingly competitive environment that now exists, transnationals will undoubtedly be resourceful enough to find alternatives to the traditional foreign investment pattern that provide reasonable bases for achieving results that are mutually advantageous to both parties.

CHAPTER FIVE

INDUCEMENTS AND GUARANTEES

Foreign investment in developing countries is affected by a wide range of incentives offered by host governments and to some extent by home governments as well. A basic issue is whether these devices significantly increase the flow of private foreign investment to the Third World and, if so, whether the resulting benefits in terms of development exceed the costs.

HOST-COUNTRY INVESTMENT INCENTIVES: TAX CONCESSIONS AND SUBSIDIES

Investment incentives offered by host countries take a variety of forms, including tax holidays during the early years of a project, rapid investment write-offs, investment credits, investment grants, loans at below-market interest rates, subsidies for training of local labor, and special provision of infrastructure such as roads, power, or housing. In addition, many types of inducements are granted for import substitution and export promotion (discussed in the section "Foreign Trade Measures"). In order to attract foreign investment, developing nations sometimes compete with each other in the generosity of their concessions and subsidies.

Although transnationals welcome and take advantage of such concessions, very few of the firms in our interview study regarded these measures as of more than marginal significance in their investment decisions. If a subsidiary is unprofitable in its early years, as is often the case, it would be unable to take advantage of tax holidays and other common forms of fiscal concessions. Moreover, as host-country conditions and priorities change, the continuation of any particular form of concession cannot be taken for granted. In addition, transnationals regard many so-called incentives as offsets to special disincentives, such as overvalued exchange rates, so that the inducements are in reality a move toward neutrality in host-government policy with regard to foreign investment.

Far more important are the "fundamentals" affecting the profitability of an operation. These include the size and growth rate of the market, the quality of the local labor force, the stability of the regulatory and administrative framework, and the soundness of the host country's general economic policies. If these conditions are satisfactory, incentive measures tend to be redundant; if the fundamentals are unsatisfactory, incentives are likely to be ineffectual. A good general rule, therefore, is that an investment climate that is conducive to domestic private enterprise will also be attractive to foreign investors even if no special inducements are offered.

Because the benefits derived by developing countries from elaborate systems of subsidies and tax concessions to attract foreign investment are unlikely to exceed their costs, developing countries would be well advised to be extremely cautious in offering such inducements. Although some incentives can be justified to compensate for the disincentives inherent in the early stages of development and for host-government policies that discourage inward flows of capital, competition among developing countries in granting special inducements to attract foreign capital may be disadvantageous to both developing countries and transnational corporations.

FOREIGN TRADE MEASURES

PROTECTION FROM IMPORT COMPETITION. Many developing countries, especially those that are relatively large in terms of population and GNP, have sought to encourage industrialization and conserve foreign exchange by providing a high degree of protection for domestic manufacturing. Among the various instruments for pursuing such import-substitution policies are steep tariffs, import quotas, prior-deposit requirements, foreign exchange allocations, and multiple currency arrangements. Brazil, for example, had for decades a Law of Similars that had the effect of prohibiting imports of products for which domestic substitutes existed.[1]

---

[1] The law was modified as part of a sweeping package of economic reforms announced on December 7, 1979.

In economic terms, protection, regardless of the form it takes, is a subsidy to domestic producers. The subsidy is financed, not by payments from the government treasury, but by direct payments from consumers to producers in the form of prices higher than those that would prevail in the absence of protection.

The countries of the Third World are concerned that transnational corporations are often in the best position to take advantage of this implicit subsidy by locating their subsidiaries behind the shelter of the protective barriers. As a consequence, the stimulus to industrialization may, in their view, provide little benefit to domestic enterprise while imposing costs on the local economy in terms of higher prices to consumers and, possibly, excessive profits for transnational affiliates insulated from foreign competition. Especially when the transnational operation consists essentially of assembly or packaging operations, the effective protection on local value added (a more accurate gauge of the extent of subsidy) tends to be much higher than the nominal rate of protection on the final product.[2]

This view constitutes a classic case of misspecification. Actually, the problem is essentially that of misguided foreign trade policies on the part of the developing-country governments rather than one of exploitative behavior on the part of transnational corporations. Given the opportunity, most foreign manufacturing firms seeking to sell in a Third World market would prefer to export from the home base rather than produce locally. The main exceptions are companies producing bulk products, such as paper goods or building materials, for which high transportation costs make shipment from the home country impractical. Companies in these fields generally neither need nor seek protection for their manufacturing in developing countries.

As we see it, import substitution has a legitimate role to play in a strategy of development. But it will best advance the host country's interest if it is a rationally designed policy in which the costs of protection are carefully weighed against the gains to be had from stimulating industrialization. The trouble with most import-substitution policies is that they are indiscriminate in choosing the industries that are accorded protection, excessive in the degree of shelter granted, too long-lasting, and overly reliant on direct controls. **In our view, a rational policy of import substitution would provide only moderate protection for a limited period and would rely mainly on measures such as tariffs, subsidies, and exchange rates that preserve the**

---

[2]/ For an illustration of the concept of effective protection, see footnote 3, p.45.

link between domestic and international prices and permit the market to perform the allocation function.

When unwise policies are followed, the costs incurred may well be unwarranted in relation to the gains, regardless of whether the firms are domestic or foreign. Moreover, excessive costs to the local economy are more likely to be reflected in *inadequate* profits than in high profits. Inadequate profits may signify that the country has been bearing the burden of subsidizing an industry that cannot possibly become competitive because it cannot produce profitably even with high protection. In the case of a firm with high profits, on the other hand, there is a presumption that protection has accomplished its purpose of nurturing an economically viable infant industry and that the time has arrived for reducing or eliminating the restrictions on imports and garnering the social benefits of the period of subsidization.

Import restrictions provide incentives only for production for the home market, not for production for export. Moreover, the restrictions typically permit the country's exchange rate to be overvalued, thereby distorting the structure of the economy away from export industries and diminishing its capacity to earn foreign exchange.

One way of countering the inherent bias of import-substitution policies against exports is to adopt export-promotion measures, such as export subsidies. In some cases, however, import restrictions and export subsidies can be reduced or eliminated through the alternative of devaluing the exchange rate.

REGIONAL ARRANGEMENTS. If a policy of import substitution is to serve its purpose of stimulating a potentially efficient industrial sector, a country must have a sufficiently large domestic market to allow economies of scale in the new industries. As measured by population and per capita GNP, many Third World markets are simply too small to warrant the establishment of industries in which scale economies are important. One escape from this dilemma is regional free-trade arrangements among groups of countries whereby complementary industries are established in each of the participating countries to serve the regional market as a whole. Adequate protection against imports from outside the region would have to be provided for a limited period.

Unfortunately, experience thus far with regional free-trade arrangements in the developing world does not provide grounds for optimism. Among the many difficulties that have beset such efforts in the past, the principal problem has been conflicts regarding the distribution of the benefits among Third World participants. **If, despite the inherent difficulties, regional economic integration arrangements could be negotiated and sus-**

tained, the broader regional market could provide attractive opportunities for transnational firms to contribute to the industrialization of developing countries.

LINKAGES TO THE DOMESTIC ECONOMY

Host governments commonly assert that certain types of foreign operations have an enclave character in the sense that they have few backward or forward linkages to the domestic economy. Backward linkages refer to a transnational's purchase of local inputs; forward linkages refer to a host country's use of the firm's output in further productive operations. Examples of inadequate backward linkages are the assembly of automobiles from imported components and the packaging of pharmaceuticals from imported materials. The export of ores or logs without further local processing into metals or plywood is an example of inadequate forward linkage. In the case of the processing of imported goods for reexport, both forward and backward linkages are generally lacking.

In various ways, Third World governments have attempted to induce closer integration of foreign operations with the local economy. They often require progressive increases in the local value-added content of manufactured products, either within the foreign affiliate or through subcontracting to local firms. Other measures with similar objectives include prohibiting the export of materials in their raw form and providing inducements for further local processing of primary materials. Host governments would also like to see transnationals make greater use of local engineering and consulting firms.

Diverse techniques are used by host governments to enforce local-content requirements. For example, preference for domestic content may be given in the awarding of the government's own purchases, in the granting of import licenses, or in the administering of government price controls.

In general, transnational firms do not have serious difficulties in adapting to local-content requirements so long as they are not pushed too far. The requirements do, however, result in higher costs and sometimes in lower quality. When companies are also expected to meet certain export targets, local-content requirements can pose serious problems because the two policies are likely to be mutually inconsistent. **Local-content requirements can help in a strategy of industrialization if they are not so extreme as to impose high costs on the economy and render the final product uncompetitive in world markets.**

Backward linkages can also be achieved through local subcontracting, a practice commonly followed by transnationals. Subcontracting often entails technical assistance in various forms, including the provision of blue-prints, specifications, tooling, training, know-how, and quality control. **We believe it is desirable for transnationals to continue to take the initiative in exploring further opportunities for local subcontracting not only as a means of serving their own interests but also as an important vehicle for transferring technology and contributing to Third World development.**

Policies to encourage forward linkages have their principal impact on extractive firms. They may take the form of host-government restrictions on the export of unprocessed primary materials or inducements for local processing. The problem is that local processing, which typically involves heavy capital outlays for facilities, may not be economically efficient. Because a country possesses a rich ore body, it does not automatically follow that on-site smelting and refining represent an efficient use of scarce capital and other resources. For this reason, **host-government regulations *mandating* local processing may not be in the long-run interest of the developing country.**

Even where investment in local processing may be internationally competitive, mandatory requirements may divert foreign investment in mining projects to other countries because of the perceived risk of heavy front-end commitments in a local environment that may be politically or economically unstable. If a host country regards local processing as essential to its long-run development strategy, it should be prepared to bear a large portion of the risk of such capital-intensive operations.

A major factor affecting the international competitiveness of locally processed materials is the conditions of access they face in the markets of industrial countries. Although raw materials often enjoy free access to foreign markets, processed materials commonly face duties and other restrictions. Even a low tariff on the processed product may imply a high degree of effective protection of the processing industry in the industrial country.[3]

Host-country inducements and requirements for local processing may in part reflect an effort to offset the artificial obstacles that processed materials face in protected foreign markets. Third World countries might find such measures unnecessary if the United States and other industrial countries gradually reduced and ultimately eliminated tariffs and other restrictions on the importation of processed products. **Although progress was made in the recently concluded multilateral trade negotiations, we recom-**

---

[3]/If the value added in processing is equal to 10 percent of the price of the processed product, a 5 percent tariff on the imported product (with raw materials entering duty-free) amounts to effective protection of 50 percent of the processing activity. This means that a 5 percent tariff enables a processing firm in the developed country to incur costs 50 percent higher than the cost of processing in the developing country.

mend further liberalization in the mutual interest of both the developing and the industrial countries.

EXPORT STIMULATION

A major goal of most non-oil-producing Third World countries is to expand their exports in order to earn the foreign exchange they need to pay for rapidly growing requirements for developmental imports, high-priced oil, and debt service. As a source of foreign exchange, exports are far more important for developing countries than inflows of public and private capital, amounting to more than twice the net inflows of capital in all forms.

Therefore, host countries seek to harness the local operations of transnational firms to their goal of export expansion. To accomplish this, they employ positive incentives such as export subsidies and favorable credit terms and negative incentives such as the denial of import licenses to subsidiaries that fail to meet specified export targets.

Although transnationals are sensitive to the need of developing countries to earn foreign exchange, many firms find specific export targets unrealistic. Production under host-government constraints such as local-content requirements often results in high costs that render impractical sales other than those to the protected home market or a more broadly sheltered regional market. Although the diseconomies of local production may be offset through various types of export subsidies, difficulties arise when neighboring countries try to realize mutually incompatible export goals and when the artificial export stimulation comes into conflict with the legitimate interests of competing producers in importing countries.

In our view, a twofold approach to dealing with these problems is the most promising: **First, it is important that the United States and other industrial countries keep their markets open to exports of those products in which developing countries are acquiring a clear comparative advantage. Second, developing countries should try to refrain from export-stimulation practices that go beyond offsetting the distortive effects of other government policies that penalize exports by raising costs, such as overvalued exchange rates and local-content requirements.** The subsidy code adopted during the recently concluded multilateral trade negotiations provides an excellent basis for the practical application of this general principle.

HOME-GOVERNMENT INDUCEMENTS TO INVEST IN THE THIRD WORLD

U.S. policy toward private direct investment in developing countries has evolved as a composite of three sets of considerations: the neutrality principle based on the view that an optimal distribution of world resources can best be achieved if the international flow of capital and other resources is allowed to respond to market forces without intervention by public authorities; the U.S. interest in promoting the economic development of low-income countries based on political, economic, and moral considerations; and the need to take into account labor's fear that private foreign direct investment entails the export of jobs from the United States to low-wage countries.

Official U.S. statements have supported private direct investment flows to the nations of the Third World. More generally, however, the official position on such outflows has wavered between the neutrality principle that "the government should neither promote nor discourage inward or outward investment flows or activities"[4] and assertions of more active encouragement of such outflows.[5]

The problem with neutrality is that it is based on the premise that in the absence of U.S. incentives or disincentives, market forces would, in fact, operate without distortion. Unfortunately, the real world is one in which host countries may offer special inducements for inward investment and in which other home governments may intervene in various ways to affect the flow of investment to foreign countries. Therefore, one interpretation of neutrality may be, not a hands-off policy, but one that seeks to neutralize existing distortions created by other countries.

Adoption of a U.S. policy of responding to foreign investment incentives and disincentives offered by other countries could lead to a spiraling of counteractions that, at substantial social cost, would leave all participants in the same positions as at the beginning. We prefer, therefore, to deal with the problem of distortion in the flow of investment through an international effort to make incentives and disincentives subject to some sort of multilateral discipline. Such an approach, although limited in scope, was adopted in 1976 in the OECD declaration and in associated decisions on transnational enterprises. It provides for disclosure and consultation when any country believes that its interests may be adversely affected by incentive or disincentive measures taken by another member country.

A case can be made for special home-country inducements for investment in developing countries because private capital flows are an important

---

[4]/Remarks of C. Fred Bergsten, former Assistant Secretary of the Treasury, at the Conference on International Trade and Investment Policy sponsored by the *National Journal*, Washington, D.C., May 11, 1979.

[5]/Letter from Reubin O'D. Askew, U.S. Special Representative for Trade Negotiations, to the U.S. Council of the International Chamber of Commerce, October 24, 1979.

supplement to public resource transfers that reflect the industrial countries' interest in contributing to development in the Third World. In practice, home governments offer few such inducements other than investment insurance. Most countries represented in our interview survey provide deferral of the tax on unrepatriated profits, but none apply this practice specifically to investment in developing countries. American companies regard tax deferral as especially significant in encouraging the reinvestment of earnings. In recent years, half the flow of U.S. direct investment to developing countries has consisted of reinvested earnings. **We favor continuation of U.S. tax deferral both because of its important contribution to the industrial countries' goal of Third World development and because the absence of deferral would place U.S. firms at a major disadvantage in relation to competing firms based in virtually all other home countries.**

The primary specific form of U.S. inducement for private investment in developing countries is the insurance and financing facilities offered by the Overseas Private Investment Corporation. For a fee, OPIC provides insurance against the risk of loss as a result of currency inconvertibility; expropriation (including "creeping" expropriation); and war, revolution, or insurrection. In addition, OPIC participates in project financing in developing countries through direct loans and credit guarantees issued to private U.S. financial institutions that provide loans to U.S. investors in Third World projects. Special consideration is given to projects in the poorest developing countries and to those sponsored by smaller American firms.

There is a sound case to be made for continuing OPIC's programs in support of private investment in the Third World. The rationale is similar to the political, economic, and moral justifications underlying public development assistance programs for developing countries. OPIC's insurance and financing programs should be viewed, not as incentives, but rather as mechanisms intended to offset some of the special disincentives to investment in the Third World. **We believe that OPIC's programs in support of investment in the Third World should be reassessed with a view to extending their scope.**

Because of the concern expressed by particular U.S. farm, labor, and industry groups with regard to Third World competition in the U.S. market, certain types of projects are excluded from OPIC financial participation either by policy or by statute. Among the exclusions or limitations are the production or processing of palm oil, sugar, or citrus crops for export to the United States and "runaway plants" (i.e., the replacement of existing U.S. facilities with a foreign plant to produce for export back to this country).

We appreciate the reasons for excluding OPIC assistance in the financing of projects to produce commodities and goods for export back to the United States in competition with domestic production. Such Third World products should not, however, also be subject to special restrictions on access to the U.S. market when they are produced abroad without benefit of unwarranted[6] government incentives or subsidies.

Official Export-Import Bank credits can facilitate private investment projects in developing countries, but their purpose is quite different from that of OPIC financing. The U.S. government has, in fact, been quite explicit in distinguishing between export credits and financial assistance for development.[7] Whereas the intention of OPIC credits is specifically to promote development through private investment, Export-Import Bank credits are designed primarily to facilitate U.S. exports.

---

[6]/See p. 46.

---

[7]/Statement by C. Fred Bergsten, former Assistant Secretary of the Treasury, before the Senate Banking Committee, May 22, 1980.

CHAPTER SIX

THE TRANSFER
OF TECHNOLOGY

The heart of the economic development process is the absorption and application of technology in its broadest sense—that is, knowledge of how to carry on useful activities and make useful things. The acquisition of technology is probably a more important element of the development process than the accumulation of capital. Indeed, the two are closely related since investment in capital equipment is an important vehicle through which new technology is introduced into an economy.

Although some rapidly growing Third World countries are beginning to generate their own technology, the developing world remains overwhelmingly dependent on the industrial countries for most of its technology. The transfer of technology is often fully packaged in the collection of resources and services associated with foreign direct investment. Increasingly, however, technology is also being made available by foreign companies in unpackaged forms through licensing agreements in which valuable knowledge and technical skill, whether patented or unpatented, are conveyed for a royalty or fee.

Developing countries express three major concerns about the process of technology transfer as it now takes place through transnational corporations: the appropriateness of the technology to the conditions prevailing in the Third World, the cost of the technology and the conditions attached to its transfer, and the extent to which an independent technological capability in the developing countries is encouraged through support for local research and development as well as for training activities.

APPROPRIATENESS OF TECHNOLOGY

The choice of technology can affect the nature and direction of development. Therefore, host countries have a legitimate concern for the appropriateness of the products and the production processes of local affiliates of transnational corporations.

PRODUCTS. With respect to products, the concern is that they may be too sophisticated, too highly designed, and too elaborately packaged to meet the needs of most of the people in poor countries. Such products, which reflect the tastes and standards of the home country, are often said to cater largely to the consumption demands of the elite in the host country.

The results of the study conducted by CED and its counterpart organizations cast some light on this subject. They show that product adaptation does take place to some extent, particularly by foreign manufacturers of consumer goods. In addition to modifications to reflect variations in tastes, customs, and climatic conditions, companies commonly alter their products to take advantage of locally available raw materials.

Outside the consumer goods field, however, product modifications tend to be minor. Pharmaceutical companies, for example, assert that they have little flexibility because drugs are the result of expensive research and require high and uniform standards of quality for their effectiveness. In the automotive and heavy-machinery industries, accessories may vary, but the basic product is standardized to facilitate interchangeability of parts and servicing worldwide. In general, market scale and cost are key considerations in determining whether to develop a new product or adapt an existing one.

Transnational as well as local firms are guided in what they produce by market demand. **To the extent that patterns of local consumption are regarded as socially undesirable, it is up to host governments to discourage such consumption, preferably through taxation rather than through direct controls or prohibitions. But if "luxury" consumption is to be discouraged, it would be appropriate to penalize it regardless of the source of the luxuries (i.e., whether imported or produced domestically by local or foreign firms).**

PROCESSES. Even more important than the appropriateness of products is the question of whether the technology embodied in production processes is compatible with the stage of development, market size, and resources of the host country. In particular, is it too capital-intensive in relation to the abundance of cheap labor in developing countries? If so, the technology could intensify the underemployment problem, aggravate inequalities of income, and worsen the balance of payments by inducing excessive importation of capital equipment.

The labor intensity or capital intensity of a country's production is as much a function of the industrial composition of its output as of the particular technology applied to individual industrial operations. The clothing and shoe industries, for example, are inherently more labor-intensive than petroleum refining or copper smelting. In some operations, moreover, little scope exists for substituting labor for capital (e.g., in extruding synthetic fibers).

In any particular industry, capital intensity may be affected by host-country policies and attitudes. Host governments frequently adopt policies that encourage the substitution of capital for labor (e.g., concessionary loans for machinery and equipment, investment tax credits, overvalued exchange rates that reduce the cost of imported capital equipment below its true market value, and restrictions on the reduction of the labor force when market demand slackens). Moreover, developing countries often resist the use of "obsolete" technologies, insisting that anything but the "latest and the best" is patronizing and offensive. **Developing countries would be well advised to be highly cautious in adopting policies that directly or indirectly promote a higher degree of capital intensity in the choice of industries or processes than is warranted by the relative costs of their resources.** Going beyond this limit on promoting capital-intensive industrialization can, in effect, slow rather than enhance the improvement in per capita standard of living in a developing country.

Process adaptation is influenced not only by host-government policies but also by the attitudes and policies of the transnationals themselves. In many of their operations in the Third World, foreign companies do modify their production processes to take into account the smaller size of markets and the availability of abundant low-wage labor. But the scope for economic adaptation of technology often turns out to be less than would seem possible at first sight. Because of low levels of skill and productivity in many developing countries, cheap labor may be expensive to use in production. Companies therefore resort to more capital-intensive processes both to reduce costs and to ensure quality, uniformity, and dependability of output. Other deterrents to technological adaptation are the substantial costs associated with developing alternative technologies and the prospect of inadequate returns on the incremental expenditure.

Nevertheless, both transnationals and host countries can take measures that could contribute to the adoption of more appropriate technologies. **We would encourage companies to establish regular procedures for considering process adaptations before technology is actually transferred. Technological exchanges among developing countries themselves are also desirable.** Such arrangements would encourage the cross-fertilization of ideas from different Third World affiliates and countries and generally raise the level of consciousness on this issue. They could facilitate not only the development of appropriate new technologies but also the consideration of older techniques and secondhand machinery that may be more compatible with the needs and resource endowments of particular Third World countries at their current stages of development.

TERMS OF TECHNOLOGY TRANSFER

PRICE. The pricing of technology is one of the most controversial aspects of the relations between transnational firms and developing countries. The basis of the conflict is a fundamental difference in perception. An extreme Third World view is that technology is part of the common heritage of mankind and that therefore, like any other form of knowledge that lies in the public domain, it should not command a price. A less extreme view is that the costs of private research and development should be largely recovered in the industrial countries and that the developing countries' more limited capacity to pay entitles them to a lower price than that charged to other purchasers. There is also a tendency to regard technology as being overpriced because it is transferred under monopolistic and oligopolistic conditions and because the expenses incurred by the transnational in developing it have already been sunk.

From the perspective of a private firm, whether transnational or domestic, the foregoing views rest on erroneous premises. Like any other investment, expenditures on research and development must yield an economic return. The return must be sufficient not only to pay for the sunk costs and risks incurred in developing the existing stock of technology but also to finance a continuing flow of new technology in the future. Because the costs of research and development are typically built into the price of the goods and services they help to produce, there is often a wide gap between the direct manufacturing cost of high-technology products and their market price—hence the perception that such products are overpriced.

Transnational firms recover their research and development costs in a variety of ways. One method is to charge royalties and fees for the sale of technology to local entities through licensing arrangements without any equity participation by the foreign company. This method is preferred by some developing countries as a way of minimizing foreign control over domestic economic activity. At the other extreme, a fully owned subsidiary may not pay separately for technology because the parent company can realize its return in the form of profits rather than payments made explicitly for the technology. When host governments set arbitrary limits on royalties or profits of foreign-owned subsidiaries, an inducement is created for a parent company to attempt to recover the costs of research and development through altering the prices on intracompany transactions—for example, charging more for components sold by the parent to its subsidiary. (See Chapter 7 for a discussion of transfer pricing.)

No simple rules can be laid down for the pricing of technology. The price of technology often varies inversely with the equity share of the supplier. Moreover, the cheapest technology may not necessarily be the most economic from the standpoint of a country's development objectives. It may be less compatible with a country's resource endowments than some alternative technology, or it may be obtainable only on terms and conditions that do not contribute as much to enhancing local capabilities through genuine absorption, diffusion, and mastery of the imported technology.

Clearly, it is in the interest of a developing country or any other prospective acquirer of technology to explore the available competitive alternatives before negotiating the terms and conditions for its acquisition. In such a negotiation, however, it would be well to bear in mind that the research and development costs of new techniques tend to be large relative to the costs of production of the goods to which they are applied. To attempt to force the transnational corporation down to its marginal cost of supplying the technology may, therefore, prevent the acquisition of the most desirable technologies and, in any case, may reduce the transnational's incentive to incur the costs of activities, such as adaptation, training, and dissemination, that would increase the contribution of the technology to the country's development goals.

CONDITIONS. Host countries are concerned not only about the price of technology but also about the restrictive conditions that may be attached to its use. Among the most important of these conditions are global or territorial restrictions on exports; tie-in clauses requiring the purchase of imports, equipment, and spare parts from the provider of the technology; and grant-back provisions giving the licensor all rights to improvements. Restrictive conditions for the use of technology may be applied by the parent firm both to local affiliates and to independent companies acquiring the technology through license or direct purchase.

Our interviews with executives of transnationals revealed various reactions to the concerns of developing countries about these conditions. Although grant-back provisions are common, it is said to be rare in practice for a reverse technological flow to occur from a licensee in a developing country back to the licensor in the home country. As for tie-in clauses, few transnationals said that they require licensees to purchase materials or components from the licensor. The exceptions tend to be in the consumer goods field, where tie-in clauses are justified as a means of quality control, especially when parent-company trademarks and brand names need to be protected.

Transnationals that limit the freedom of foreign affiliates or licensees to export products embodying the acquired technology do so as a means of controlling or preventing competition with other affiliates or licensees of the same parent company. This type of restriction is probably the most objectionable from the standpoint of developing countries because it runs counter to their virtually universal policy of encouraging exports as an essential element of their development strategy.

In comparison with firms based in other countries, American transnationals are subject to home-country constraints on the restriction of exports. U.S. antitrust law, applied extraterritorially, prohibits most attempts by American transnationals to include such restrictions in licensing agreements with nonaffiliated companies. Market allocation agreements with fully controlled subsidiaries are, however, generally permitted.

Although we do not favor the extraterritorial application of U.S. law, we agree with the principle that companies *not under the common control of a parent firm* should refrain from engaging in restrictive practices such as allocating markets or limiting exports. This principle has been incorporated in a set of voluntary guidelines on restrictive business practices recently negotiated by the United States and other countries under the auspices of the United Nations.

REDUCING TECHNOLOGICAL DEPENDENCE

Because developing countries often regard foreign technology as inappropriate, high priced, and subject to restrictive conditions, they seek to reduce their technological dependence on foreign companies. But the desire for greater technological independence has a broader psychological and political basis. Even Western European countries were preoccupied in the 1960s with the problem of their alleged technology gap in relation to the United States, partly for economic reasons but also because the gap was viewed as implying excessive dependence and therefore as a threat to their sovereignty.

The quest of the developing countries for greater technological independence has two aspects: the desire for a research and development capability and the insistence that foreign technology in its broadest sense be adequately mastered, absorbed, and diffused within a host country through the employment and training of local technical and management personnel.

RESEARCH AND DEVELOPMENT. It has been estimated that only about 1 percent of the total R and D expenditures of transnationals occur in the Third World.[1] The low volume of R and D activity in developing countries is self-reinforcing. Third World scientists and engineers trained at local universities and technical schools tend to migrate to the industrial countries, and many of those trained at foreign universities do not return home. This "brain drain" is due not only to the higher salaries offered abroad but also to other advantages such as wider contacts, more ample facilities and equipment, and greater opportunities for publication.

There are several reasons why most transnationals with affiliates in the Third World have not established R and D facilities there: the economies of scale of centralized research and development, the small size of local markets, the absence of skilled manpower and a scientific and technical infrastructure in most developing countries, and the desire to avoid a duplication of effort.

However, many foreign companies have established local facilities in developing countries for testing products, adapting them to local conditions, controlling quality, and more generally, technical trouble-shooting. The scale and diversity of those activities depend on the size and growth rate of the local or regional market. **Where transnational firms already conduct extensive local operations involving product adaptation and testing, we recommend that serious consideration be given to their potential for further development into applied-technology centers.**

A number of developing countries have established, or are seeking to establish, R and D facilities in local universities or research institutions. American transnationals have expressed strong support for these efforts, and a number of non-U.S.-based firms contribute to them financially or technologically. These facilities can be mutually beneficial, especially in generating and promoting technology oriented toward the adaptation of both products and processes to domestic conditions. **We endorse the idea of U.S. companies contributing to indigenous research institutions and recommend that additional forms of cooperation be explored such as the local subcontracting of technological services.**

---

[1] Thomas N. Gladwin and Ingo Walter, *Multinationals Under Fire* (New York: John Wiley, 1980), p. 484.

EMPLOYMENT AND TRAINING. Another means by which developing countries seek to pursue their industrialization goals with less dependence on foreign firms is through the indigenization of the local operations of transnational companies. To this end, host governments often limit the number and type of foreign nationals that may be employed and lay down regulations for the training and upgrading of the local labor force.

In most cases, company self-interest and host-country policies of indigenization coincide in the fields of employment and training. With few exceptions, transnationals prefer to employ and train host-country nationals not only for unskilled and skilled manual jobs but for all levels, including technical, financial, and managerial positions.

The trend toward the employment of host-country nationals as managers and technical personnel reflects an increased awareness on the part of transnational companies of the financial and other costs of employing nonlocal personnel. Not only is it costly to transport and maintain home-country nationals for these positions, but such assignments may not be particularly welcome to executives, who may regard them as outside the mainstream of career development. When nonlocal personnel are used, it is frequently because qualified nationals are not available and need to be trained. **We believe that arbitrary host-country limits on the use of home-country personnel are generally unnecessary and ill advised.**

In order to promote the employment of local managerial and technical personnel, transnationals provide a wide range of training programs. In addition to on-the-job training and the use of "mature" subsidiaries as instruction centers, companies send local employees to domestic and foreign universities. Companies also conduct their own special training programs or make use of local and regional management training facilities such as the Fundação Getulio Vargas in Brazil, the Singapore Institute of Management, or the Asian Institute of Management in Manila. **We believe that out-company training programs in the Third World are in the mutual interest of host country and transnational enterprise and recommend that the companies contribute to strengthening them through financial and personnel support.**

58

CHAPTER SEVEN

FINANCIAL ASPECTS
OF FOREIGN
DIRECT INVESTMENT

Developing countries have expressed concern about several of the financial aspects of the foreign investment relationship. Given the foreign exchange stringency that confronts most Third World countries in the course of their development, it is only natural for them to be preoccupied with the balance-of-payments effects of the operations of transnational firms. Certain specific implications of the way in which transnationals finance their operations are also worrisome: the effects of borrowing in the host country on the supply of capital for local entrepreneurs and the effects of borrowing by foreign affiliates from their parent companies on the affiliates' tax liability to the host country. Finally, host countries are troubled by what they regard as the widespread opportunities for circumventing domestic law and regulation through the manipulation of transfer prices on intracorporate transactions.

BALANCE-OF-PAYMENTS EFFECTS

Foreign direct investment in developing countries is sometimes condemned on the grounds that it "takes out more than it puts in." The idea that foreign investment results in a net drain of foreign exchange from the poor countries is based on a comparison of two sets of annual financial flows: the outflow of earnings from affiliates in the developing countries to the transnationals in the form of dividends, interest, royalties, and fees and the net inflow of equity and loan capital from the transnationals to affiliates in the host countries.

The first point to be made is that any assessment of the effects of transnational operations in the Third World must rest on much broader considerations than their balance-of-payments effects. The more basic issue (as explained in Chapter 2) is the contribution of the corporation to the gross domestic product of the host country and the proportion of the claims to that product that remains within the host country.

With respect to the narrower question of the balance-of-payments effects, it is true that an excess of outflows of earnings over inflows of new capital has long been a feature of the direct foreign investment relationship with the developing world. This pattern holds whether one examines the relationship with transnational companies worldwide or only with those based in the United States. In 1978, for example, U.S. companies received slightly under $7 billion of interest, dividends, royalties, and fees from affiliates in the developing world while providing new capital of only $3.1 billion in the form of equity and loan investments by the parent firm.[1]

However, a simple comparison of these two flows does not make sense. In the first place, the two are logically unrelated. The outflow of earnings in a given year is related to the cumulative investment during prior years, not to the inflow of capital in the same year. In the second place, the balance-of-payments effects on the host country cannot be judged by comparing one item of foreign exchange receipts (capital inflows) with one item of payments (remittances of earnings). Instead, it is necessary to take into account the impact of foreign investment on all components of a country's balance of payments, particularly the effect on the volume of imports and exports.

In the case of natural resource investment, for example, the bulk of the output is typically exported, contributing to net foreign exchange receipts on the trade account. In the case of investment in manufacturing, however, the situation is different. Although there has been a steady growth in the value of exports of manufactures by affiliates of U.S. companies in the developing world,[2] the bulk of manufacturing is for the host-country market. Even in this case, however, the balance-of-payments effects on the trade account may be positive if the production saves foreign exchange by substituting for imports that would have occurred in the absence of the investment. It is apparent, therefore, that when the trade effects, as well as capital flows and earnings, are taken into account, the situation becomes far too

[1]/Both figures are net of reinvested earnings of $2.9 billion. Obie G. Whichard, "U.S. Direct Investment Abroad," *Survey of Current Business*, U.S. Department of Commerce, July 1979, pp. 16 and 22.

[2]/ Deepak Nayyar, "Transnational Corporations and Manufactured Exports from Poor Countries," *The Economic Journal* 88 (March 1978).

complex for broad generalizations about the balance-of-payments consequences of foreign direct investment. Moreover, as we noted earlier, the basic effects of the transnational relate less to the balance of payments than to its impact on the long-term productive resources and technological capabilities of the host country.

TRANSNATIONAL FINANCING OF HOST-COUNTRY OPERATIONS

BORROWING LOCALLY. Only about one-eighth of U.S. foreign investment is financed directly through loans and equity capital from U.S. sources.[3] The rest is raised in the host country or from such sources as the Eurocurrency market or is generated by the affiliates themselves from retained earnings and depreciation.

To the extent that foreign firms rely on local financing, they are said not only to diminish their contribution of capital and foreign exchange to the host economy but also to have detrimental effects on local enterprise. Because domestic capital is usually in short supply in developing countries, borrowings by foreign firms may deprive local projects of their only source of financing.

Our interview survey revealed that the transnational practice of raising capital from local sources is widespread. Although some firms share equity in their subsidiaries with one or two local partners or more widely with individual investors in the host country, the more frequent pattern is to borrow locally. Such borrowing is less common among extractive firms because few developing countries have capital markets capable of providing the large sums required for extractive operations.

The principal reason for local borrowing is the minimization of risk, especially the foreign exchange risks of inconvertibility and/or depreciation of the local currency. Local financing through the sharing of equity is sometimes resorted to as a means of lessening the risk of nationalization. With ownership partly in the hands of host-country nationals, expropriation may be less likely, and the owners may be more fully compensated if it does occur.

It would seem that raising capital locally would deprive domestic enterprises of financing by reducing the volume or increasing the cost of available funds. However, transnationals cite a number of offsetting considerations: host-government regulations that limit foreign access to domestic capital markets, the increase in the willingness of foreign banks to lend to

---

[3] U.S. Department of Commerce, *Survey of Current Business*, July 1975, p.31.

domestic projects because of the confidence inspired by the local operations of transnational firms, and limitations on profit repatriation which create a pool of surplus funds that transnationals invest both short and long term within the host country.

If individual developing countries believe that the volume of local borrowing by transnationals is detrimental to domestic enterprise, they have the option of setting limits on foreign access to local capital, as many have already done. In considering restrictions on local borrowing, host governments would presumably want to take into account not only the short-run direct effects on the supply of funds but also the longer-term indirect effects on the volume of foreign investment and the related opportunities created for local enterprise.

BORROWING FROM THE PARENT COMPANY. Foreign affiliates may receive loans from their parent companies. A number of developing countries have been concerned that such transactions can constitute a form of local tax avoidance because interest paid on a loan is normally regarded as a deductible expense, whereas profit on an equity investment is taxable.

In general, transnational firms recognize the potential for abuse in treating interest on parent-company loans as a business expense, particularly the temptation to use excessive interest charges as a way of achieving the tax-free transfer of profits. One method commonly used by host countries to control such practices is a withholding tax on interest paid by affiliates to parent companies. Some developing countries limit the amount of interest that can be paid or have enacted legislation making interest nondeductible for tax purposes.

We believe it is legitimate for host countries to concern themselves with practices associated with intracompany lending. One method of regulating such practices is the establishment of reasonable ceilings on debt/equity ratios beyond which debt would be treated as equity for local tax purposes. Another is to treat as equity those loans from the parent firm that exceed some specified maturity. If host countries adopt regulations of this kind, it is incumbent on them not to levy excessive taxes on the profits of foreign affiliates.

TRANSFER PRICING

The term *transfer pricing* refers to the pricing of goods and services in transactions between related firms. A substantial proportion of a foreign affiliate's purchases and sales are transactions with the parent company or its other affiliates. Critics contend that the transfer prices in such intracompany transactions often diverge from the arm's-length prices that would prevail through the working of market forces if the parties to the transaction were unrelated.

Transnational manipulation of transfer prices is said to reflect attempts to shift income between jurisdictions in order to minimize taxes or circumvent host-government regulations. For example, companies may adjust intracorporate import and export prices in order to shift earnings from countries with high taxes on profits to those with low taxes. To reduce payments of import duties to a host country, transfer prices on imported products bearing high tariffs may be reduced; conversely, transfer prices may be *raised* on imported goods in order to circumvent price controls on final goods based on production costs or to offset restrictions on royalties on research and development, on charging administrative expenses to foreign affiliates, or on the repatriation of profits.

Few of the transnationals in our survey admitted to the use of manipulative transfer pricing. Most claimed to be guided in their intracorporate pricing by established principles applied in a standardized manner (e.g., use of competitive external prices or a cost-plus formula when external markets for similar products or services did not exist). It was also noted that local shareholders would object to manipulative transfer pricing and that sacrifice of profitability of individual affiliates would run counter to company policy of motivating the management of subsidiaries by regarding each as a profit center.

Those companies that do use special transfer prices said the practice is rarely followed for the purpose of avoiding Third World taxes. Adjustment of transfer prices is, rather, intended to ensure a reasonable profit when host-country limitations are placed on product prices, royalties, administrative charges, and profit remittances. According to a number of companies, if unreasonable restrictions of this sort were removed, the incentive to adjust transfer prices for these purposes would be reduced.

As a general policy, we endorse the principle included in the OECD Guidelines for Multinational Enterprises that enterprises should "refrain from making use of the particular facilities available to them, such as transfer pricing that does not conform to an arm's-length standard, for modifying in ways contrary to national laws the tax base on which members of the group are assessed."[4] By the same token, it is important that host countries refrain from imposing excessive and inequitable taxes on foreign affiliates.

---

[4] Organization for Economic Cooperation and Development, Guidelines for Multinational Enterprises, *International Investment and Multinational Enterprises* (Paris: OECD, 1976), p. 16.

Many host countries monitor prices in intracorporate transactions by comparing them with prices for comparable external transactions. The main problem in monitoring transfer prices occurs in the case of charges for technology, administrative services, and the like because the allocation of joint costs differs from company to company. Some help in this connection might be obtained from the Technology Information Exchange System (TIES), a clearinghouse on technology contracts maintained by the United Nations Industrial Development Organization (UNIDO).

Many home-country tax authorities, including the U.S. Internal Revenue Service, already have stringent rules on transfer pricing, including acceptable norms for allocating joint costs among parts of a transnational enterprise. Unfortunately, these norms sometimes conflict from country to country and can result in double taxation of some corporate revenues. **Collaboration between host and home countries in establishing and monitoring rules on the allocation of joint costs would help to avoid jurisdictional disputes.**

CHAPTER EIGHT

THE SCOPE FOR
INTERNATIONAL ACTION

Because transnational corporations operate on a global scale, national regulation of their activities can be supported and supplemented by action at the international level. Among the most important international initiatives are the negotiation of codes of conduct for transnational operations, improving the bargaining capabilities of host countries, creating facilities for the exchange of information relevant to the foreign investment relationship, and strengthening the mechanisms for dispute settlement.

CODES OF CONDUCT

The purpose of an international code of conduct is to set down comprehensive and generally acceptable standards for the behavior of transnationals and for their treatment by host and home governments.

OECD GUIDELINES. The industrial countries reached agreement on such a code in 1976 under the auspices of the OECD. It is intended to maximize the transnational contribution to host countries and reduce areas of conflict. The agreement, which applies to both private and state-owned enterprises, includes voluntary guidelines for transnational enterprises, recognizes the responsibility of host and home governments to treat domestic and foreign-owned firms in an equitable manner, and encourages the establishment of machinery for the settlement of disputes.

The OECD guidelines also endorse such general principles as respect for the host country's economic and social aims and priorities and the avoidance of illicit payments to public officials. Additional provisions relate to disclosure of information, restrictive business practices, transfer pricing, employment and industrial relations, and transfer of technology.

The OECD guidelines, which were revised and strengthened in 1979, constitute the first set of multilateral rules on the subject of transnational enterprises applying to countries beyond a strictly regional grouping. They reflect a recognition by the major home countries of the desirability of international standards of behavior in this field. With the encouragement of industry associations and home governments, many corporations have declared adherence to the guidelines, and it is expected that host governments will increasingly look to the guidelines in the formulation of their own policies toward transnational enterprises. **We urge companies to declare their willingness to observe the OECD guidelines if they have not already done so.***

U.N. CODE. Much slower progress is being made in the negotiation of a worldwide code of conduct under the auspices of the United Nations Commission on Transnational Corporations and its staff support agency, the U.N. Centre on Transnational Corporations (UNCTC). This complex exercise is directed especially toward the operation of foreign enterprises in developing countries. Although addressing essentially the same range of subjects included in the OECD agreement, the drafts of the various parts of the U.N. code include far more detail and reflect a much more ambitious attempt at standard setting. On three subjects, the U.N. code would, in effect, incorporate the results of major separate negotiations: On employment and labor, the code would refer to the standards in the International Labour Office (ILO) Tripartite Declaration; and on restrictive business practices and transfer of technology, it would include the results of two separate negotiations now at different stages of completion in the United Nations Conference on Trade and Development (UNCTAD).

Because national economic and social objectives differ among sovereign states, the main responsibility for policy regarding transnational enterprises must continue to reside with host countries and to be reflected in *national* laws, regulations, and practices. Nevertheless, we believe that a constructive role can be played by the negotiation of general *international* guidelines relating to the operations of transnationals. The negotiations themselves serve as an educational process by highlighting points of consensus as well as areas in which further efforts at conflict resolution are required. Moreover, the standards of good behavior incorporated in the codes can provide points of departure for national legislation and regulation tailored to the situation and needs of individual host countries.

---

*See memorandum by MARK SHEPHERD, JR., page 70.

We believe that the basic principles underlying the OECD guidelines should be incorporated in any universal codes relating to transnational enterprises. Specifically, we endorse the following elements: voluntary standards rather than legally binding commitments; recognition of responsibilities of both governments and transnationals; application of guidelines to all international investors, whether private, state-owned, or mixed companies; and inclusion of the principle of respect for international law and national treatment once a foreign enterprise is established. However, nothing in the principles should limit the right of governments to regulate the entry of foreign-controlled enterprises.

BILATERAL AGREEMENTS. In years past, the United States succeeded in negotiating with a number of industrial countries bilateral treaties of friendship, navigation, and commerce that included commitments relating to international investment. Although no comparable reciprocal agreements of a legally binding nature have been negotiated with individual developing countries, the United States is beginning to follow this approach, currently working out an agreement with Singapore and preparing to do so with Egypt. Moreover, several European countries, including Germany, Switzerland, and the Netherlands, have been actively pursuing such efforts with some success.

The bilateral agreements, although limited in scope in comparison with the U.N. effort, cover many of the main areas of potential conflict between home and host governments. For example, the draft U.S. agreement with Singapore is based on four main principles: Established investments will receive national or most-favored-nation treatment, whichever is more favorable; international law regarding expropriation will apply, and compensation will be prompt, adequate, and effective; capital and profits will be freely transferable; and specific mechanisms will be provided for dispute settlement.

Because individual governments have primary responsibility for setting policy on transnational corporations, such bilateral U.S. investment treaties can be an effective means of codifying standards of behavior. **We urge the U.S. government vigorously to pursue a program of bilateral investment treaties with developing countries.**

IMPROVING THE BARGAINING CAPABILITIES OF HOST COUNTRIES

In addition to coordinating the negotiations on a code of conduct, U.N. member governments have given UNCTC a mandate to conduct programs to strengthen the negotiating capacity of developing countries in their dealings with foreign firms.

Through advisory services, particularly to smaller and poorer developing countries, the Centre assists in the formulation or revision of laws and regulations pertaining to transnationals, including national screening, monitoring, and incentive mechanisms. The Centre also helps host countries to examine policy options on key issues in the relations between foreign corporations and host countries, including such alternative forms of corporate and contractual arrangements as joint ventures, licensing or management contracts, and production-sharing arrangements.

In addition to such general advice, the Centre provides staff support to host governments for specific negotiations with transnationals, including the analysis and review of draft agreements. The Centre also conducts extensive training programs in developing countries. These programs consist of general workshops on regulation of, and negotiation with, transnationals and workshops focused on specific economic sectors and issues. The primary purpose of these activities should be to help establish a climate of law and regulation that will attract foreign investors and at the same time maximize their contribution to the social and economic development of host countries.

In order to ensure a balanced and pragmatic approach to the provision of technical services, the Centre should make a special effort to staff these activities with individuals who have practical experience in actual operations of, and negotiations with, both host countries and transnational enterprises. **We recommend that the private business sector cooperate with the U.N. Centre on Transnational Corporations by making legal, technical, and financial personnel available for short-term assignments to assist in its training and advisory services.*** This cooperation could foster a mutual understanding of the legitimate aspirations of both parties.

INTERNATIONAL INFORMATION SYSTEMS

Another means of strengthening the bargaining position of developing countries is to improve their knowledge of the operations of transnational corporations. Two agencies of the United Nations are establishing information systems for this purpose.

UNCTC is developing a wide-ranging information network. Its main areas of interest are legal information, including the policies and laws of host and home governments with regard to transnationals; trends in transnational activities, such as the stock, flow, and pattern of direct investment; industrial analyses of sectors of particular interest to developing countries; information on specific corporations, including general data on groups of companies and material on leading companies in given sectors; and infor-

---

*See memorandum by MARK SHEPHERD, JR., page 70.

mation on specific aspects of transnational operations such as financial practices, market structures, and technology. The Centre also collects and analyzes contracts and agreements between foreign corporations and host governments.

UNIDO, headquartered in Vienna, is also in the process of creating its own information systems. Its two programs partly overlap that of UNCTC. UNIDO's Industrial and Technological Information Bank (INTIB) is designed to aid host countries in selecting appropriate technology by providing information on technological alternatives, suggesting criteria for selecting among them, and offering information on the implications of the terms of contracts and the unpackaging of technology. In addition, UNIDO has established TIES, which is a clearinghouse for information from host governments on the terms of technology contracts.

Our interviews revealed that many companies have serious doubts about such information systems. They argue that developing countries would not be able to learn much from a technology information bank. According to the companies, the problem is, not finding information on alternative technologies, but choosing applicable solutions from the great mass of information already available.

With regard to a system that records the terms of negotiated contracts, the firms point out that such contracts are tailored to fit specific situations. It is unclear whether the terms of a contract negotiated with one country could serve as a guide for another country. Companies are also critical of the duplication of effort in the monitoring of company contracts by both UNCTC and TIES.

Transnationals are also concerned about the type and volume of information that goes into these systems. Companies are worried that the information may not be accurate or complete and that there are inadequate safeguards to protect confidential or proprietary information. In addition, they feel that not enough importance is given to cost considerations and the need for selectivity.

Although markets function best when knowledge is fullest, these points raise important questions about international information systems. *It is desirable for the U.S. business community to participate more actively in the design and functioning of U.N. information systems on transnationals so that existing shortcomings can be corrected or taken into account when the systems are used.**

DISPUTE SETTLEMENT

Various international facilities exist for the settlement of investment disputes. Perhaps the best known is the World Bank's International Centre

---

*See memorandum by MARK SHEPHERD, JR., page 70.

for the Settlement of Investment Disputes (ICSID), which provides machinery for arbitration, conciliation, and fact-finding. Although eighty-four countries are signatories to the ICSID Convention, none is from Latin America. The refusal of Latin American countries to sign is based on the Calvo principle, which maintains that disputes with foreign companies should be settled solely under national jurisdiction and within the judicial processes of the host country.

It is impossible to know with any precision how extensively investment contracts have incorporated provisions for the use of ICSID or how effective ICSID has been in settling disputes. Governments that have agreed to the terms of the convention are not bound to include provision for the use of ICSID facilities in individual investment agreements with transnational enterprises. Even where such provisions have been included, copies of the agreements need not be filed with ICSID. The lack of a significant number of proceedings under ICSID may be more a reflection of the facility's deterrent effect on the impairment of contracts than of a reluctance to make use of the facility.

Other facilities for international dispute settlement include the ICC Court of Arbitration, the Permanent Court of Arbitration in the Hague, and such regional facilities as the arbitration centers in Kuala Lumpur and Cairo under the aegis of the Asian-African Legal Consultative Committee. Adjudication of disputes is often facilitated by fact-finding procedures that may then provide the basis for solutions through the application of generally accepted principles of international law.

We urge the inclusion of provisions for international dispute settlement in agreements between host governments and transnational enterprises. If such a precaution is taken at the outset, even if it is limited to independent fact-finding, it can help to avoid subsequent costly and disruptive disputes.

MEMORANDA OF COMMENT, RESERVATION, OR DISSENT

Pages 5 and 30, by HENRY B. SCHACHT

It should be underscored that "refrain from" in this section means that United States affiliates should never bribe public officials or yield to extortion. To do so would be wrong and would undermine the essential ideal of trust that should exist between public officials and the people they represent.

Page 7, by JACK F. BENNETT

Rather than suggesting that import substitution and local-content requirements advance development, this statement should, in my opinion, have pointed out that such practices are likely to harm the economies of the countries concerned.

Pages 12 and 65, by MARK SHEPHERD, JR.

The OECD Guidelines for Multinational Enterprises, if strictly interpreted, could lead to the disclosure of information considered proprietary by many corporations.

Pages 12 and 67, by MARK SHEPHERD, JR.

The problem with this proposal is that it does not seem in the best interests of transnational corporations, since they would be subsidizing the future ability of the developing countries to challenge them.

Pages 12 and 68, by MARK SHEPHERD, JR., with which J. PAUL LYET has asked to be associated

The report concedes that "many companies have serious doubts" about such information systems, as they certainly should. Important reservations about such systems include their possible inaccuracy, lack of timeliness, lack of utility, and problems of privacy. It would be extremely difficult to assure companies that safeguards to protect unpublished information would be adequate. In addition, it is not likely that sensitive information (possibly the most useful data in the eyes of the developing countries) would be made available to such a "public" information system. As the report points out, "markets function best when information is fullest." But markets change quickly. Much time and effort could be expended in developing elaborate institutionalized information systems, only to find that they answer *yesterday's* questions.

Page 31, by HENRY B. SCHACHT

United States' leadership in discouraging foreign corrupt practices should be exercised through *unilateral* action as well as through bilateral and multilateral agreements. Although unilateral action may be ineffective, the essential point is that as a society, we wish our citizens to conduct themselves according to certain ethical standards and to accept the consequences of so doing because we believe that how we act is as important as what we achieve.

APPENDIX A

NOTES ON *FOREIGN ENTERPRISE IN DEVELOPING COUNTRIES*
by Dr. Isaiah Frank (The Johns Hopkins University Press, 1980)

This policy statement, *Transnational Corporations and Developing Countries: New Policies for a Changing World Economy,* is based in large part on the results of a major study on the role of transnational enterprise in the Third World sponsored by CED and its counterpart organizations in Australia, France, Germany, Japan, Sweden, and the United Kingdom.[1] The study has been published by The Johns Hopkins University Press as a CED supplementary paper, *Foreign Enterprise in Developing Countries.*

The role of transnational enterprise in the developing world has long been a subject of controversy. Against a backdrop of the prevailing criticisms, the study sought the views of company executives on patterns of foreign ownership and operations, national and international financing, trade policies, technology transfer, investment incentives, and a variety of other economic, political, and social issues. The purpose was to clarify the problems and opportunities of operating a business in developing countries and to examine ways in which existing difficulties might be resolved to mutual advantage.

The study was based on in-depth interviews with top management personnel of ninety transnational firms headquartered in the countries represented by the collaborating organizations and in other nations. An effort was made to obtain a cross section of firms based on the criteria of size and industry group of the parent firms, geographic distribution of Third World affiliates, size of the host-country market, stage of development of the host country, and percentage of affiliates' equity owned by the parent firm.

Each participating company was initially asked to prepare a confidential factual questionnaire on each of its subsidiaries in a developing country. The purpose was to facilitate examination of the responses to the interview questions in relation to the type and location of subsidiaries controlled by the parent firm.

---

[1] Committee for Economic Development of Australia (CEDA); Institut de l'Entreprise (IDEP), France; European Committee for Social and Economic Progress (CEPES), Germany; Keizai Doyukai (KD), Japan; Business and Social Research Institute (SNS), Sweden; and Policy Studies Institute (PSI), Great Britain.

The interviews with senior executives were the heart of the study. Each was based on a questionnaire consisting of forty-eight questions, many with multiple parts, designed to elicit reactions to the principal concerns expressed by developing countries about the operations of transnationals. In order to ensure coverage of the main issues as perceived by the developing countries, drafts of the questionnaire were informally reviewed by staff members of United Nations agencies concerned with these problems.

Through the interviews, the candid opinions and attitudes of knowledgeable executives with responsibility for operations of Third World affiliates were sought, and complete confidentiality of the replies was guaranteed. In order to encourage a frank discussion of the issues, the invitation to participate explicitly stated that official company views were not being sought because we hoped to avoid formal responses prepared or reviewed by companies' public information or legal departments.

In most cases, the interview questionnaire was sent to the firms well in advance of the interview in order to allow the executives ample time to think about the subjects raised and to plan for the presence of the appropriate people at the interview.

The interviews were carried out over a three-year period from mid-1976 to mid-1979; most were conducted during 1978. An average of three company executives participated in an interview. But in the case of the American firms, for example, as many as thirteen people took part in a single interview. The average length of the interviews was slightly more than four hours.

Each collaborating organization prepared a summary of the responses of all its participating firms to each interview question. These summaries and, in most cases, the reports on the individual interviews were sent to CED for analysis and synthesis.

Drafts of the study were reviewed by a number of experts, including staff members of the United Nations Centre on Transnational Corporations, who provided an extensive critique.

APPENDIX B

THE CHANGING DIMENSIONS OF U.S. DIRECT INVESTMENT IN DEVELOPING COUNTRIES

This appendix presents a quantitative examination of the scope and trends in U.S. private foreign direct investment in the Third World. A summary discussion of this subject is included in Chapter 2.

LIMITATIONS OF THE DATA

What is commonly understood by private foreign direct investment is the flow of equity and loan capital from parent to affiliate. However, in using data on direct investment, it is important to be aware of several significant limitations.

UNDERSTATEMENT OF FINANCIAL FLOWS. The measure of the flow of financial resources (including reinvested earnings) understates the size of the flows for which the parent is responsible. For example, a loan to a foreign subsidiary from a nonaffiliated home-country (or third-country) bank would not be included in direct foreign investment, even though the transaction may depend on the reputation or formal guarantee of the parent company.

OMISSION OF OTHER RESOURCE FLOWS. A more important limitation is the fact that foreign direct investment does not necessarily reflect the flow of other resources (technology, management, and marketing services) from parent to affiliate. Yet, an increasing proportion of the activities of transnational enterprises in developing countries takes forms that are not necessarily related to financial flows from parent to subsidiary but that may nevertheless imply some degree of control by the foreign company—for example, management contracts, technical assistance agreements, and production-sharing arrangements. In light of these trends, the conventional measures of direct investment must be viewed as lower-bound indicators of the scope of the foreign activities of transnational corporations.

CRITERION FOR DETERMINING DIRECT INVESTMENT. Apart from the neglect of nonfinancial flows of resources, two other problems arise in attempting to measure direct investment originating not only in one country but also in the developed countries as a group. The first concerns the criterion for determining what constitutes private direct investment as opposed to portfolio investment. Some measure of central control by the parent company is an essential part of the definition of direct investment; therefore, the problem is to give quantitative expression to this condition in terms of the required minimum percentage of equity ownership. The United States, Germany, and Sweden apply the standard of at least 10 percent; France, 20 percent; Australia, 25 percent. In the cases of the United Kingdom and Japan, strictly defined percentages are apparently not applied. Of course, any fixed threshold for equity is arbitrary, but the lack of uniformity of practice among home countries compounds the problem of aggregation.

EFFECTS OF INFLATION AND EXCHANGE RATE CHANGES. The second difficulty in combining national data is the problems inherent in converting them into a single currency under conditions of inflation and fluctuating exchange rates of the type experienced during the last few years. Aggregates expressed in terms of the U.S. dollar are seriously affected by changes in the value of the dollar relative to the currencies of other investor countries, and because aggregate data on foreign investment are generally expressed in dollars, the effects of exchange rate changes should be kept in mind. For example, in mid-May 1978, the German mark had appreciated 72.6 percent in terms of the dollar compared with its pre-June 1970 parity. Expressed in dollars, therefore, the book value of the total stock of U.S. and German direct investment abroad would have increased even if no new net flows had taken place over this period. Moreover, the proportion of German compared with U.S. investment has risen substantially.

FLOW OF DIRECT INVESTMENT TO DEVELOPING COUNTRIES

Private foreign direct investment in the Third World has increased sharply in current dollars since 1960 (Table B-1). The average annual flow from all industrial countries, including the United States, was $6,198 million during the six-year period from 1972 to 1977. This flow was three times as great as the average for the 1960-to-1965 period. A comparably strong upward trend since 1960 is shown when the U.S. investment flow is considered separately. From 1972 to 1977 it averaged $2,614 million annually, or more than 40 percent of total direct investment flows to developing countries from industrial countries.

When the data on flows are expressed in constant dollars, however, a substantially weaker rising trend emerges. Whereas the average flow between 1972 and 1977 was three times that in the 1960-to-1965 period in current dollars, it was not quite twice that of the earlier period in constant dollars.

TABLE B-1

Annual Average Net Flow of Private Direct Investment to Developing Countries[a] from Industrial Countries[b]

(millions)	1960–1965		1966–1971		1972–1977[c]	
	All Countries	United States	All Countries	United States	All Countries	United States
Current dollars	$1,790	$786	$2,892	$1,539	$6,198 ($7,213)	$2,614 ($3,571)
Constant 1970 dollars[d]	2,093	946	3,011	1,609	3,763 (4,379)	1,679 (2,307)

[a] The figures in the table are based on data published by the OECD. The OECD includes in the category of "developing countries" the lower-income nations of southern Europe (Spain, Portugal, Greece, Turkey, Yugoslavia, Cyprus, Malta, and Gibraltar).

[b] Includes Australia, Austria, Belgium, Canada, Denmark, France, Germany, Italy, Japan, the Netherlands, New Zealand, Norway, Sweden, Switzerland, the United Kingdom, and the United States. Also included is the Commission of the European Economic Community. The figures include reinvested earnings.

[c] Figures in parentheses omit 1974. A change in the manner in which a U.S. petroleum company reported the liabilities of a foreign branch had the net effect of reducing the U.S. investment stock for the years 1966 to 1975. The effect was greatest in 1974 as a result of the large increase in oil prices, royalties, and tax rates. Because annual flows essentially reflect the difference between the stock of investment in successive years, the data on flows of investment show a major discontinuity in 1974. For further details, see Obie G. Whichard, "U.S. Direct Investment Abroad in 1976," *Survey of Current Business*, U.S. Department of Commerce, August 1977, pp. 40-47.

[d] Constant dollars are calculated on the basis of price deflators provided by the OECD for the total flow of resources to developing countries.

SOURCES: Organization for Economic Cooperation and Development: *Development Assistance*, 1961–71 issues (Paris: OECD, 1962–72); *Development Cooperation*, 1972–78 issues (Paris: OECD, 1973–79); *The Flow of Financial Resources to Less-Developed Countries, 1956–63* (Paris: OECD, 1964).

The trend in direct investment flows is strongly affected by certain accounting changes in the U.S. data that had a particularly sharp impact in 1974. As shown by the parenthetical figures in Table B-1, the elimination of that year results in substantially higher average flows from 1972 to 1977.

One of the most interesting facts shown in Table B-2 is the growing importance of the flow of U.S. private direct investment to the Third World compared with the volume of official development assistance. Whereas direct private investment was less than one-fourth as great as official development assistance from 1960 to 1965, the two categories had become approximately equal by 1978, each constituting about 37 percent of the U.S. total.

Another fact that emerges clearly from the table is that when all types of private flows are combined (whether for all the industrial countries or for the United States alone), they exceed by a wide margin the flow of official resources to the Third World. This reflects in particular the marked upward trend in private portfolio investment in the form of bank loans.

SOURCE OF FOREIGN DIRECT INVESTMENT

At the end of 1977, the stock of U.S. direct investment in the developing world was just under $40 billion (Table B-3). About half the flows in recent years consisted of reinvested earnings.[1]

The United States is by far the largest source of direct investment in the Third World, accounting for 47 percent of the total *stock* of such investment in 1977. As shown in Table B-3, however, the U.S. proportion has been on a declining trend; *flows* in recent years from the United States have amounted to only 42 percent of the total from all sources.

The decline in the proportion of foreign direct investment originating in the United States has been accompanied by other noteworthy shifts in origin. A comparison of stock and flow data in the last two columns of Table B-3 shows that the shares of the United Kingdom and France have also been declining, whereas the shares of Germany and Japan have been increasing. The most dramatic change has occurred in the case of Japan. Although its cumulative stock of direct investment in the Third World was less than 7 percent of the total from all sources at the end of 1977, its average flow over the preceding six years was more than 11 percent of the total.

In making comparisons by country of origin, however, the caveat about the effect of exchange rate changes should be kept in mind. Because the data in Table B-3 relate to amounts expressed in dollars, the trend differences by country of origin are partly attributable to the depreciation of the pound and the appreciation of the mark and the yen in terms of the dollar.

---

[1] Based on data for 1977 and 1978 in Obie G. Whichard, "U.S. Direct Investment Abroad in 1978," *Survey of Current Business*, U.S. Department of Commerce, July 1979, pp. 24 and 25.

TABLE B-2

Share of Various Flows in Total Net Flow[a] of Resources from Industrial Countries[b] to Developing Countries

(percent)	1960–1965		1966–1971		1972–1977		1978	
	All Countries	United States	All Countries	United States	All Countries	United States	All Countries	United States
Official development assistance	60.7	70.0	49.5	59.2	38.5 (36.5)[c]	40.4 (36.5)	28.5	37.2
Direct investment	19.7	16.9	21.6	27.1	20.1 (21.9)	28.5 (34.7)	16.4	36.9
Private portfolio investment and export credits	13.2	7.2	19.4	5.8	28.1 (27.9)	16.6 (14.8)	44.4	21.2
Other[d]	6.4	5.9	9.5	7.9	13.3 (13.7)	14.5 (14.0)	10.7	4.7
Total	100.0	100.0	100.0	100.0	100.0(100.0)	100.0(100.0)	100.0	100.0

[a] Excludes grants by private voluntary agencies.

[b] See Table B-1, note b, for list of countries.

[c] Parenthetical figures exclude 1974; see Table B-1, note c, for explanation.

[d] "Other" includes other official flows and multilateral portfolio investment.

SOURCES: Organization for Economic Cooperation and Development: *Development Assistance, 1961–71 issues* (Paris: OECD, 1962–72 issues (Paris: OECD, 1962–72); *Development Cooperation, 1972–79 issues* (Paris: OECD, 1973-80); *The Flow of Financial Resources to Less-Developed Countries, 1956-63* (Paris: OECD, 1964); Development Assistance Committee, *Flows of Resources to Developing Countries, 1961–71* (Paris: Development Assistance Committee, July 24, 1973).

TABLE B-3

Share of Private Foreign Direct Investment in Developing Countries, by Country of Origin: Stocks and Flows

	Stock at Year-end 1977 (millions of U.S. dollars)	Flow, 1972–1977 (annual average)	Stock at Year-end 1977 (percent of total)	Flow, 1972–1977 (percent of total)
United States	$39,766	$2,614	46.8	42.2
Japan	5,662	707	6.7	11.4
Germany	6,816	753	8.0	12.2
United Kingdom	12,118	695	14.2	11.2
France	5,543	257	6.5	4.1
Other[a]	15,142	1,169	17.8	18.9
Total	$85,047	$6,195	100.0	100.0

[a] "Other" includes Australia, Austria, Belgium, Canada, Denmark, Italy, the Netherlands, Norway, Sweden, and Switzerland.

SOURCES: Organization for Economic Cooperation and Development: *Stock of Private Direct Investments by DAC Countries in Developing Countries, End 1967* (Paris: OECD, 1972); *Development Cooperation, 1971–78* issues (Paris: OECD).

DISTRIBUTION OF U.S. DIRECT INVESTMENT, BY HOST COUNTRY

As shown in Table B-4, U.S. direct investment in the Third World is overwhelmingly concentrated in Latin America in terms of both total stock and current flows. Brazil is by far the largest host to U.S. investment in the developing countries, accounting for almost $8 billion of a total of $48 billion. Mexico, Panama, and Venezuela rank after Brazil as major recipients.

Outside Latin America, the main recipients of U.S. investment are Indonesia and the Philippines in Asia and Libya and Nigeria in Africa. Except for the Philippines, U.S. investment in these countries is highly concentrated in petroleum.

The negative investment figures for the Middle East are largely explained by the fact that the fixed investment in petroleum, entered in the data at historical cost, is now more than offset by the liabilities of certain major U.S. companies to the oil-producing countries for royalties and taxes based on increased petroleum prices. There has also been disinvestment because oil companies have been forced to liquidate equity positions in favor of service contracts and other arrangements.

When the data on flows and stocks in the last two columns of Table B-4 are compared, it becomes apparent that the concentration of U.S. direct investment in Latin America has been accentuated in recent years and that a notable decline has occurred in Africa's share of the total.

SECTORAL DISTRIBUTION OF U.S. DIRECT INVESTMENT

A summary picture of the distribution of U.S. investment abroad by sector is given in Table B-5. Manufacturing is the most important field of U.S. foreign investment in developing countries, accounting for $16 billion of the total stock of $48 billion. Moreover, its share of the total has been growing in recent years at the expense of the shares of mining and smelting and petroleum. Within manufacturing, chemicals and machinery are the principal categories.

One of the most interesting features of the data is the rapidly growing share of U.S. investment in the "other" category, a trend that is dominated by the rapid increase in investment in finance and insurance. The stock of investment in this category, amounting to more than $12 billion at the end of 1979, was heavily concentrated in offshore financial centers such as Bermuda, the Bahamas, and Panama. It includes assets not only in branches of U.S. banks but in financial affiliates of U.S. petroleum and other nonbanking companies.

TABLE B-4

Share of U.S. Private Foreign Direct Investment in Developing Countries, by Destination: Stocks and Flows[a]

(millions of dollars)

	Stock at Year-end 1979	Flow, 1973–1979 (annual average)	Percent of Total	
			Stock at Year-end 1979	Flow, 1973–1979 (annual average)
Africa	$ 3,615	$ 153	7.6	4.0
Latin America and Caribbean	36,834	3,141	77.0	83.4
Brazil	7,514	750	15.7	19.9
Mexico	4,575	363	9.6	9.6
Panama	2,756	204	5.8	5.4
Venezuela	2,206	-5	4.6	-0.1
Middle East	-375	-174	-0.8	-4.6
Asia and Oceania	7,766	646	16.2	17.2
Total	**$47,840**	**$3,766**	**100.0**	**100.0**

[a] The data in this and following tables are not strictly comparable to the data in Tables B-1 and B-2 because of differences between the OECD and the U.S. Department of Commerce in categorizing the lower-income countries of southern Europe as either "developed" or "developing" nations.

SOURCES: U.S. Department of Commerce, *Selected Data on U.S. Direct Investment Abroad, 1966–76* (Washington D.C.: U.S. Government Printing Office, 1977); Obie G. Whichard, "U.S. Direct Investment Abroad in 1979," *Survey of Current Business*, U.S. Department of Commerce, August 1980, pp. 16–36.

TABLE B-5

Sectoral Shares of U.S. Private Direct Investment in Developing Countries

(millions of dollars)

	Stock at Year-end 1979	Flow, 1973–1979 (annual average)	Percent of Total	
			Stock at Year-end 1979	Flow, 1973–1979 (annual average)
Mining and smelting	$ 2,416	$ 23.0	5.1	0.6
Petroleum	7,231	82.3	15.1	2.2
Manufacturing	16,198	1,388.6	33.9	36.4
Total	25,845	1,493.9	54.0[a]	39.2
Other[b]	21,996	2,317.8	46.0	60.8
Finance and insurance[c]	[12,178]	[1,467.8]	[25.5]	[38.5]
Total	**$47,841**	**$3,811.7**	**100.0**	**100.0**

[a] Percent total has been rounded to nearest whole number.

[b] Includes transportation, communication, public utilities, trade, finance and insurance, and other industries. The greater part of investment in finance and insurance represents transactions in offshore financial centers.

[c] Included in "Other" above.

The declining U.S. direct investment position in petroleum is evidenced by a comparison of the stock and flow data in Table B-5. It is explained by the factors mentioned in connection with the negative investment figures for the Middle East in Table B-4.

INCOME ON U.S. FOREIGN DIRECT INVESTMENT

Of total income (including reinvested earnings) averaging more than $31 billion earned by foreign affiliates of U.S. companies in 1978 to 1979, affiliates in developing countries accounted for almost $11 billion, or approximately 35 percent (Table B-6). In current dollars, income earned in the developing countries increased by more than 280 percent since the period from 1966 to 1971. In constant dollars, however, the increase was only 94 percent. This tapering off was particularly marked in the more recent period; average income from 1978 to 1979 from the developing countries was only 30 percent higher than the average for the 1972-to-1977 span.

Throughout this period, petroleum has been the largest source of U.S. investment income in the developing world. But its share has been declining, having fallen from an annual average of 56 percent of the total between 1966 and 1971 to 43 percent in the period from 1978 to 1979. On the other hand, the share of total income earned from investment in manufacturing in the developing countries has risen over the same period from 16 percent to 20 percent.

Rates of return on the stock of manufacturing investment can be calculated by dividing income by the direct investment position. As shown in Table B-7, the rate of return on investment in the developing countries was approximately 15 percent in 1978 and 1979.[2] In 1979, the rate of return from U.S. manufacturing investment in the developed countries was substantially higher. Because of the special factors affecting the recent data on the investment position in the two remaining sectors, petroleum and "other," similarly calculated rates of return for those categories would be meaningless.[3]

FEES AND ROYALTIES

Income from foreign operations is received by U.S. companies not only in the form of interest, dividends, and reinvested earnings but also in the form of fees and royalties for the transfer of technology, use of trade-

---

[2] Because the rate of return is an average for existing investment, it may not be indicative of the profitability of new investment. This was particularly true in 1978, when the depreciation of the dollar resulted in increased income but affected the book value of total investment only marginally.

---

[3] See pp. 75, 80, and Table B-1, note c, p.76

TABLE B-6

Income[a] on U.S. Foreign Private Direct Investment, by Source

(millions of dollars)	Annual Average		
	1966–1971	1972–1977	1978–1979
Developing Countries			
Current dollars	$ 2,839	$ 6,552	$10,850
Petroleum	1,588	3,346	4,698
Manufacturing	452	1,145	2,153
Other	799	2,061	3,999
Constant 1970 dollars[b]	2,980	4,441	5,795
Petroleum	1,665	2,318	2,490
Manufacturing	472	776	1,157
Other	843	1,347	2,148
Developed Countries			
Current dollars	3,824	9,988	20,209
Constant 1970 dollars	3,982	6,831	10,774
Total			
Current dollars	6,663	16,540	31,059
Constant 1970 dollars	$ 6,962	$11,272	$16,569

[a] Income is composed of interest, dividends, and reinvested earnings of incorporated affiliates, plus the earnings of unincorporated affiliates.

[b] Constant dollars for the years 1961 to 1977 are calculated on the basis of price deflators provided by the OECD. The deflators for 1960, 1978, and 1979 are derived from the U.S. producer price index for all commodities.

SOURCES: Organization for Economic Cooperation and Development, *Development Cooperation*, 1973 and 1978 issues (Paris: OECD); U.S. Council of Economic Advisers, *Economic Indicators* (Washington, D.C.: U.S. Government Printing Office, November 1979); U.S. Council of Economic Advisers, *Economic Report of the President, 1979* (Washington, D.C.: U.S. Government Printing Office, 1979); Obie G. Whichard, "U.S. Direct Investment Abroad in 1979," *Survey of Current Business*, U.S. Department of Commerce, August 1980, pp. 16–36.

marks and copyrights, and the provision of management and other services (Table B-8). Annual earnings in the latter forms in the developing countries averaged $895 million from 1978 to 1979, and the trend in current dollars has been sharply upward since the 1966-to-1971 period. In constant dollars, however, only a modest rise of 21 percent occurred in the annual average of fees and royalties received between the 1966-to-1971 period and the 1978-to-1979 period.

Broadly speaking, earnings in the form of fees and royalties have amounted to about 8 percent of the amounts earned in developing countries in the form of interest, dividends, and reinvested earnings. That figure must be regarded, however, as an understatement of the quantitive relationship between the flow of technological, managerial, and related services, on the one hand, and the flow of capital, on the other. The reason is that in practice, the two flows cannot be separated. An investment that finances the importation of capital goods by an affiliated company is at the same time contributing to the stocks of capital and technology because some new technology is almost invariably "embodied" in capital equipment. More broadly, the typical pattern of foreign direct investment is to supply capital and "disembodied" technological and managerial services in a single pack-

TABLE B-7

Income and Rate of Return[a] on U.S. Foreign Private Direct Investment in Manufacturing, 1977 and 1978

(millions of dollars)	Income	Rate of Return (percent)	Income	Rate of Return (percent)
Developing countries	$ 2,019	15.2	$ 2,287	15.0
Developed countries	$ 8,554	15.1	$11,359	17.9
Total	$10,573	15.1	$13,646	17.3

[a] Income divided by the average of the year-beginning and year-end direct investment positions. See also Table B-5, note a.

SOURCE: Obie G. Whichard, "U.S. Direct Investment Abroad in 1979," *Survey of Current Business,* U.S. Department of Commerce, August 1980, p. 22.

age. Some of the services of such technology and management are often paid for separately in the form of royalties and fees. But host governments do not always permit such payments, especially to parents of wholly owned affiliates. In those cases, the compensation for technological and managerial services is, in effect, included in profits and appears in the statistics as earnings on capital rather than as royalties and fees.

TABLE B-8

Fees and Royalties on U.S. Foreign Private Direct Investment, by Source

(millions of dollars)	Annual Average		
	1966–1971	1972–1977	1978–1979
Developing Countries			
Current dollars	$ 381	$ 619	$ 895
Petroleum	76	159	225
Manufacturing	126	182	207
Other	179	278	463
Constant 1970 dollars[a]	399	422	483
Petroleum	79	107	121
Manufacturing	132	126	112
Other	188	189	250
Developed Countries			
Current dollars	1,114	2,426	3,928
Constant 1970 dollars	1,165	1,640	2,085
Total			
Current dollars	1,495	3,045	4,823
Constant 1970 dollars	$1,564	$2,062	$2,568

[a]Constant dollars for the years 1961 to 1977 are calculated on the basis of price deflators provided by the OECD for the total flow of resources to developing countries. The price deflators for 1960, 1978, and 1979 are derived from the U.S. producer price index for all commodities.

SOURCES: Organization for Economic Cooperation and Development, *Development Cooperation*, 1973 and 1978 issues (Paris: OECD); U.S. Council of Economic Advisers, *Economic Indicators* (Washington, D.C.: U.S. Government Printing Office, July 1980); U.S. Council of Economic Advisers, *Economic Report of the President, 1979* (Washington, D.C.: U.S. Government Printing Office, 1979); Obie G. Whichard, "U.S. Direct Investment Abroad in 1979," *Survey of Current Business*, U.S. Department of Commerce, August 1980, pp. 24–25.

OBJECTIVES OF THE COMMITTEE FOR ECONOMIC DEVELOPMENT

For thirty-five years, the Committee for Economic Development has been a respected influence on the formation of business and public policy. CED is devoted to these two objectives:

To develop, through objective research and informed discussion, findings and recommendations for private and public policy which will contribute to preserving and strengthening our free society, achieving steady economic growth at high employment and reasonably stable prices, increasing productivity and living standards, providing greater and more equal opportunity for every citizen, and improving the quality of life for all.

To bring about increasing understanding by present and future leaders in business, government, and education and among concerned citizens of the importance of these objectives and the ways in which they can be achieved.

CED's work is supported strictly by private voluntary contributions from business and industry, foundations, and individuals. It is independent, nonprofit, nonpartisan, and nonpolitical.

The two hundred trustees, who generally are presidents or board chairmen of corporations and presidents of universities, are chosen for their individual capacities rather than as representatives of any particular interests. By working with scholars, they unite business judgment and experience with scholarship in analyzing the issues and developing recommendations to resolve the economic problems that constantly arise in a dynamic and democratic society.

Through this business-academic partnership, CED endeavors to develop policy statements and other research materials that commend themselves as guides to public and business policy; for use as texts in college economics and political science courses and in management training courses; for consideration and discussion by newspaper and magazine editors, columnists, and commentators; and for distribution abroad to promote better understanding of the American economic system.

CED believes that by enabling businessmen to demonstrate constructively their concern for the general welfare, it is helping business to earn and maintain the national and community respect essential to the successful functioning of the free enterprise capitalist system.

Trustee On Leave For Government Service

STATEMENTS ON NATIONAL POLICY
ISSUED BY THE RESEARCH AND POLICY COMMITTEE

PUBLICATIONS IN PRINT

High Employment Without Inflation:
   A Positive Program for Economic Stabilization *(July 1972)*

Reducing Crime and Assuring Justice *(June 1972)*

Military Manpower and National Security *(February 1972)*

The United States and the European Community *(November 1971)*

Improving Federal Program Performance *(September 1971)*

Social Responsibilities of Business Corporations *(June 1971)*

Education for the Urban Disadvantaged:
   From Preschool to Employment *(March 1971)*

Further Weapons Against Inflation *(November 1970)*

Making Congress More Effective *(September 1970)*

Training and Jobs for the Urban Poor *(July 1970)*

Improving the Public Welfare System *(April 1970)*

Reshaping Government in Metropolitan Areas *(February 1970)*

Economic Growth in the United States *(October 1969)*

Assisting Development in Low-Income Countries *(September 1969)*

*Nontariff Distortions of Trade *(September 1969)*

Fiscal and Monetary Policies for Steady Economic Growth *(January 1969)*

Financing a Better Election System *(December 1968)*

Innovation in Education: New Directions for the American School *(July 1968)*

Modernizing State Government *(July 1967)*

*Trade Policy Toward Low-Income Countries *(June 1967)*

How Low Income Countries Can Advance Their Own Growth *(September 1966)*

Modernizing Local Government *(July 1966)*

Budgeting for National Objectives *(January 1966)*

Educating Tomorrow's Managers *(October 1964)*

Improving Executive Management in Federal Government *(July 1964)*

---

*Statements issued in association with CED counterpart organizations in foreign countries.

CED COUNTERPART ORGANIZATIONS
IN FOREIGN COUNTRIES

Close relations exist between the Committee for Economic Development and independent, nonpolitical research organizations in other countries. Such counterpart groups are composed of business executives and scholars and have objectives similar to those of CED, which they pursue by similarly objective methods. CED cooperates with these organizations on research and study projects of common interest to the various countries concerned. This program has resulted in a number of joint policy statements involving such international matters as energy, East-West trade, assistance to the developing countries, and the reduction of nontariff barriers to trade.

CE   Círculo de Empresarios
            Serrano Jover 5-2°, Madrid 8, Spain

CEDA   Committee for Economic Development of Australia
            139 Macquarie Street, Sydney 2001,
            New South Wales, Australia

CEPES   Europäische Vereinigung für
            Wirtschaftliche und Soziale Entwicklung
            Reuterweg 14,6000 Frankfurt/Main, West Germany

IDEP   Institut de l'Entreprise
            6, rue Clément-Marot, 75008 Paris, France

経済同友会 Keizai Doyukai
            (Japan Committee for Economic Development)
            Japan Industrial Club Bldg.
            1 Marunouchi, Chiyoda-ku, Tokyo, Japan

PSI   Policy Studies Institute
            1-2 Castle Lane, London SW1E 6DR, England

SNS   Studieförbundet Näringsliv och Samhälle
            Sköldungagatan 2, 11427 Stockholm, Sweden